GREAT WESTERN
KINGS

C.J. Freezer

Foulis

ISBN 0 85429 426 0

A FOULIS Railway Book

First published 1984

© **Winchmore Publishing Services Limited 1984**

Published by:
Haynes Publishing Group Ltd
Sparkford, Yeovil,
Somerset BA22 7JJ

Distributed in USA by:
Haynes Publications Inc.
861 Lawrence Drive,
Newbury Park,
California 91320, USA

Produced by:
Winchmore Publishing Services Limited,
40 Triton Square
London NW1 3HG

Printed in Spain
by Graficromo s.a.

Further titles in this series will be published at regular intervals. For information on new titles please contact your bookseller or write to the publisher.

Titles in the *Super Profile* series:

BSA Bantam (F333)
MV Agusta America (F334)
Norton Commando (F335)
Honda CB750 sohc (F351)
Sunbeam S7 & S8 (F363)
BMW R69 & R69S (F387)

Austin-Healey 'Frogeye' Sprite (F343)
Ferrari 250GTO (F308)
Fiat X1/9 (F341)
Ford GT40 (F332)
Jaguar E-Type (F370)
Jaguar D-Type & XKSS (F371)
Jaguar Mk 2 Saloons (F307)
Lotus Elan (F330)
MGB (F305)
MG Midget & Austin-Healey Sprite (except 'Frogeye') (F344)
Morris Minor & 1000 (ohv) (F331)
Porsche 911 Carrera (F311)
Triumph Stag (F342)

Contents

Enter a King

For the last forty years of Great Western steam, the 'Kings' were the acknowledged flagships of the locomotive fleet, the express passenger machines par excellence. During the whole of this time, any loco spotter worthy of the name wished, avidly, to record every one of them in his notebook; after all, there were only thirty of them altogether, and they were confined to a few well-known routes.

As the unmistakable front end of a 'King' came into view in the distance, pulses began to beat faster. It was not difficult to pick out one of these machines. The sheer bulk of the locomotive was one pointer, although to the experienced eye this was not conclusive. At a distance one might be mistaken, for all GWR front ends bore a strong family resemblance to one another. However the curved steam pipes, characteristic of the GW four-cylinder layout, confirmed one's suspicions, for both the 'Stars' and the 'Castles' had a slimmer look about them.

It was the unique leading bogie which gave it away, with its part-outside, part-inside framing. It wasn't necessary to wait until the cross-beam was visible, the absence of glint from the leading wheel treads was the key. Of course, this characteristic was shared by the remaining 4-4-0s of the 'Duke' and 'Bulldog' classes, but any loco spotter who confused one of these venerable antiques with a 'King', from any angle, under any lighting conditions, was not fit to stand at the end of a platform.

When it became obvious that it was a 'King', the gaze moved upwards over the bufferbeam, in the hope of seeing that tell-tale golden glint of the presentation bell that told you that this was the cop of cops, No 6000, *King George V*, the first of the class, and the

Left: The great grandfather of the 'Kings', the first de Glehn compound 4-4-0 at the Mulhouse Collection.
Above: The Great Western *King George V*, No 6000, as originally produced at Swindon in 1927.

locomotive that – according to GWR propaganda at all events – took all the honours at the Fair of the Iron Horse during the centenary celebrations of the Baltimore & Ohio Railway in 1927. When this was seen, all but the most sedate and unemotional of loco spotters, a breed not noted for iron self-control, was apt to send

notebook, pencil and ABC flying in sheer excitement.

The 'Kings' were magnificent machines, of that there is no doubt. Anyone who questions this should see *King George V*, happily preserved at Hereford. They were the largest 4-6-0s on British metals, and one of the largest and most powerful of the type ever built. They were superbly proportioned and, almost to the very end, kept in immaculate condition. The ever-eager publicity machine at Paddington exploited them for all

they were worth, and in this respect alone, the 'Kings' surely earned their keep. They were the greatest, the ultimate, name your superlative, and it fits.

Yet, as one looks back, one small doubt remains. Why were there only thirty? Why were there only two batches, and one replacement? Why, after 1930, was all new passenger locomotive construction confined to the older, smaller, 'Castle' class? Was the crown gilt rather than gold?

Let us consider the evidence.

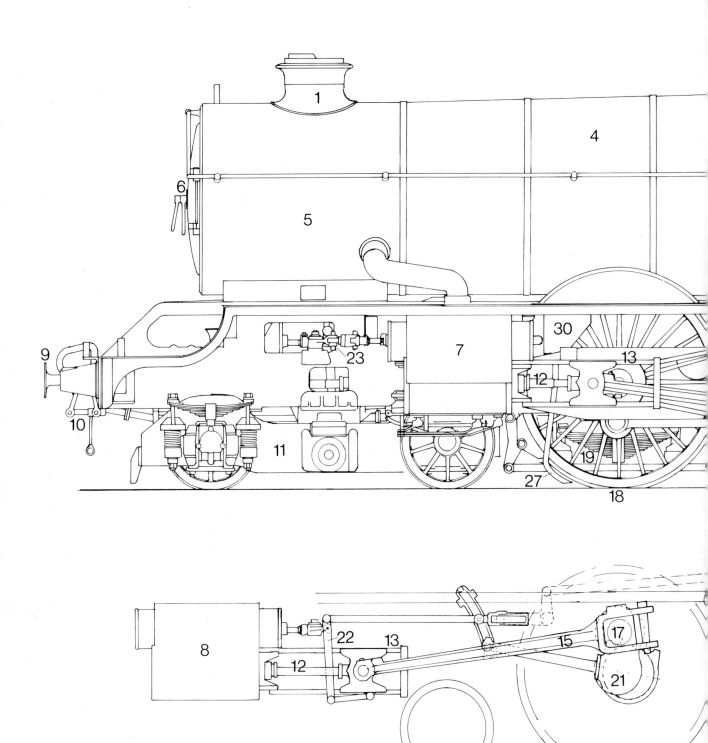

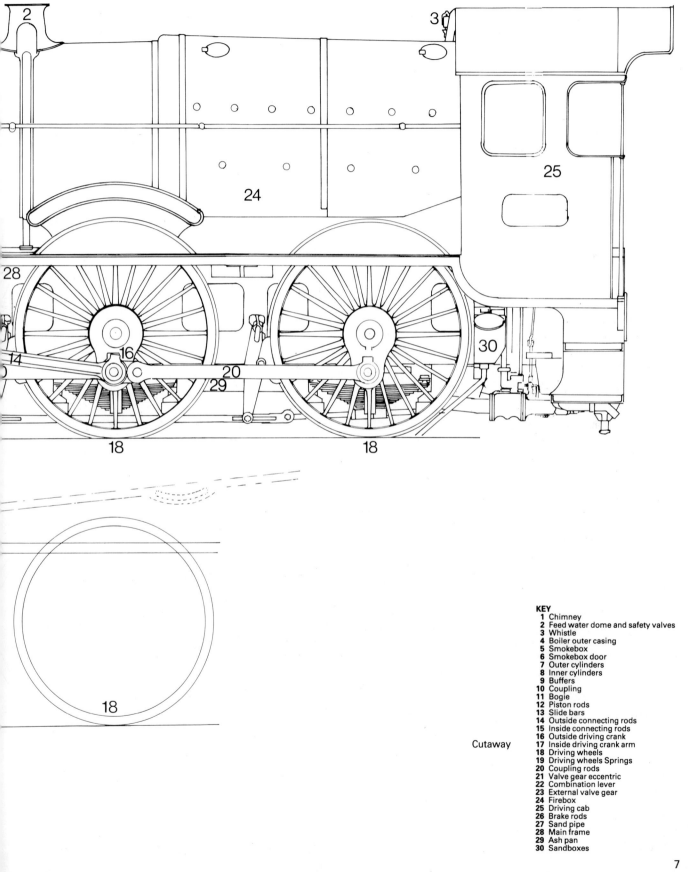

Cutaway

The Origins of the Design

The 'Kings' were the final stage of GWR four-cylinder locomotive development. Since there were only four distinct types of GWR four-cylinder locomotives, one of which comprised a solitary locomotive, this doesn't seem to be saying much, but in practice, there was more to it than at first appears. GWR locomotive history has a fairly closely-knit pattern, and it is easier to distinguish the steps that led to the production of the 'Kings' if we begin, not in the 1920s, but at the turn of the century.

It was a different world; to see this it is sufficient to look at what Paddington Station was like in those days. The structure of the station was quite different; there were only three arched roofs over the train shed, only now were the platforms being extended beyond the end of the shed. But above all, both the trains and the locomotives themselves were from another world.

The coaches were almost entirely made up of clerestory stock, they were panelled and painted in a most elaborate style. The locomotives fell into three groups. There were the ubiquitous saddle tanks, part and parcel of the GWR scene and, only slightly modified with a more distinctive square section saddle tank, were to be a part of the scene down to the end of steam. Then there were the elegant single drivers, a few of the old 'Queen' class, but mainly the graceful 7 ft 8 in (2.34 m) 'Dean Singles', most of which still carried their glorious boilers with that magnificent polished brass dome. There were also some of the 'Badmintons', four-coupled with beautiful sweeping curves and double frames.

There were others gaunt and ungainly, with ugly boilers devoid of a dome, sporting the awkward foreign belpair firebox and above all with stark, straight frames. It seems incredible that these machines were designed by the man responsible for the flowing lines of the other engines, but we are told in the columns of *The Locomotive*, that they are the work of Mr Dean. Which only goes to show that it is not a good idea to believe everything that appears in print.

Mr Dean, nearing the end of his tenure of office, was a figurehead. Those florid locomotives, with the voluptuous curves usually associated with the style of the 1890s may have been his idea, but the details were probably the work of the drawing office. It is a sound, workmanlike style gloriously embellished in accordance with contemporary thought on aesthetics. The later versions showed the growing influence of Mr Dean's bright young second-in-command, Mr Churchward, a man of strong character with an enviable talent for selecting sound schemes. He had some very clear ideas on the future of GWR motive power and was busy trying some of them out.

At this stage, the most important developments were centred on the boiler. It is a truism to say that the success or failure of a steam locomotive depended on the boiler design. It was not unduly difficult to determine the size and configuration of the cylinders, the underlying mathematics are completely straightforward. There were some problems on the chassis, however; for example, it took a long time to get that outside-framed leading bogie, such a characteristic feature of all the current express passenger locomotives on the GWR, to run properly, and the initial designs showed a marked propensity to come off the track. One experimental locomotive built in the 1880s is reputed to have come

off so often on its first attempt to get out of the erecting shops, that it was dragged back ignominiously, placed under tarpaulins until it was decided how best to re-use the parts and, in the best traditions of the Victorian age, it was never spoken of again.

However, boiler design was still something of an esoteric art. This was particularly true of locomotive boilers, which operated on a principle completely different from all other types.

Unlike stationary and marine boilers, which at the time could be large and massive, a locomotive boiler was limited in size. It had to handle wildly-fluctuating demands for steam, whereas with other steam plants the demand was fundamentally constant. These two factors led to the development of a design that could both generate steam rapidly and within reasonable limits vary the output to keep pace with demand.

The initial multi-tubular design first fitted to the 'Rocket' proved more than adequate for the job and various attempts to provide something even better ended inconclusively. However, it was soon appreciated that the proportions – not merely of the boiler barrel and the numbers of tubes but of the firebox, smokebox, blastpipe and chimney – were critical.

Nowhere was this better appreciated than on the Great Western Railway. It is assumed that in providing a long, almost level run out of Paddington, Brunel gave Daniel Gooch and his successors a perfect stretch of railway. In practice he handed them a monumental headache. Not only has the road a slight but palpable upgrade, but for much of the time trains are heading upwind; if the boiler was unable to provide enough steam, the trains were unable to make much headway.

On the GWR there was never any division between the design and manufacture of locomotives

Near the end of its life, No 6022 *King Edward III* has its last overhaul at its Swindon birthplace in October 1955.

and their operation. Although there was not as close a link at Swindon as existed at Wolverhampton, every promising engineer was expected to spend part of his youth in the running sheds, finding out how the designs fared in service. It was an invaluable arrangement and ensured that, by the time a man got to a position to influence locomotive design, he was not only fully familiar with GWR practice, but also had a clear understanding of the true function of a locomotive: to haul trains on time, at a profit.

By the time he became Mr Dean's principal assistant, George Jackson Churchward was aware that loads were increasing and that more and more powerful locomotives would be needed. He set about experimenting, and the first fruits were to be seen on the 'Atbaras'. These 4-4-0s differed from the preceding 'Badmintons' in two important ways. First, the frames lost their ornate curves; they were not functional, and were weaker than the straight-framed

pattern finally adopted. Second, and equally alarming to the railwayac of the day, the boiler lost its high dome and gained a box-like firebox. At the same time, a drumhead smokebox sitting on a saddle replaced the older style. There was a strong American influence at work here; one advantage of this arrangement was that the boiler was now a separate unit, which could easily be removed. It was the start of the GWR boiler standardisation scheme as we understand it today, but to a large extent this was only a logical development of existing practice.

The straight barrel boiler soon gave place to a tapered pattern, and became the Standard No 2. A larger version, the No 4, was developed and married to the basic 'Atbara' frames to become the 'City' class. Churchward was moving towards another classification structure, which would bring the various locomotives into orderly groups based on common design parameters, but not necessarily

absolute identity. Of rather greater importance was the fact that he was trying to move towards common load haulage capacity and route availability.

Dean finally left office in 1902. Churchward took over and unveiled his plans, a complete range of radically different locomotives, based on an entirely novel cylinder arrangement. For the first time, the GWR moved to outside cylinders and at the same time waved goodbye to double frames, low slung footplates and every facet of Victorian steam locomotive design. The clerestory roof disappeared from the coaches; a modern image was being created.

This is no place to explore the full implications of the Churchward plan – the first example in Britain of a concerted, connected range of locomotives intended to meet all needs for the next twenty years – we are solely concerned with the large passenger classes.

The prototype was No 100 (later No 2900), a gaunt, unlovely 4-6-0, which appeared with a completely parallel precursor of the most important boiler Swindon produced, the No 1; but any pretensions to looks were completely destroyed by the deep bufferbeam. This was deliberate, for it was originally intended to fit No 100 with 5 ft 8½ in (1.72 m) diameter wheels as the prototype of a range of general purpose 4-6-0s. These were not to appear until 1937 and No 100 (initially named *Dean*, then *William Dean*) remained a large wheeled locomotive and, although officially incorporated into the 'Saint' class, was always the odd man out.

The first true standard 4-6-0 was No 98, later No 2998 and initially, and very appropriately called *Vanguard*, although later it was renamed *Ernest Cunard* to commemorate a member of the Board of Directors. It had a part-tapered boiler, and was the forerunner of a succession of substantially similar locomotives. From the outset they proved to be fast, powerful machines, clearly among the best express passenger locomotives in the world, although to contemporary eyes they were ugly and showed too much American influence.

At this time, the attention of the locomotive world was focused on the Nord railway's de Glehn compounds. Unlike most of the breed, these were not only efficient but fast. Since express trains were still the fastest form of transport on earth in Edwardian times, this was important and the compound principle was given the credit.

Churchward was able to order a de Glehn compound for trials, No 102, *La France*, a modified version of the Nord 4-4-2s, built to fit the GWR loading gauge.

The second standard 4-6-0, No 171, was similar to No 98 but had 225 psi boiler pressure to bring it into line with the French machine. It was named *Albion* and a little

later, to make comparison more accurate, was converted to a 4-4-2.

Although the performance of the French compound apparently showed no marked advantage over the GWR two-cylinder designs, its behaviour was sufficiently good to persuade the company to obtain two more, this time following a slightly larger design currently in use on the Nord. Nos 104 and 105 arrived in 1905, and were later named *President* and *Alliance.*

In the meantime, Churchward had looked at the cylinder layout and found it good. In its final form, the de Glehn system involved outside cylinders driving on the second axle and inside low-pressure cylinders driving on the leading axle. The divided drive spread the power over two sets of hornblocks, but as the two engines on each side of the locomotive were opposed, a reasonably good reciprocating balance was achieved.

Accordingly, a further experimental locomotive was constructed, using the same general layout and boiler as the two-cylinder machines, but with four-cylinder divided drive. As with the two-cylinder machines, a long stroke in proportion to the bore was adopted, coupled with long-travel valves. No 40 also had an ingenious version of Walschaerts valve gear, which took its drive, not from an eccentric or return crank, but from the opposing crosshead.

The new locomotive, which was named *North Star,* appeared in 1906. It proved a complete success, for the multi-cylinder drive materially improved the riding qualities of the machine. It is not generally appreciated that, quite apart from any other side effects, a rough riding locomotive puts up a very variable performance for a very simple, if rather subtle reason.

A steam locomotive is a relatively simple device capable of extremely complex control.

Moreover, its power output is determined by the ability of the fireman to put coal into the firebox in the right place and the right time. If the footplate is attempting to simulate the behaviour of a small trawler in a choppy sea, not only will nine out of ten drivers hold back, but much more to the point, 99 out of every 100 firemen will be unable to throw coal through the firehole fast enough to make steam in a quantity.

This was the key to the de Glehn's speed; not that the locomotive possessed some esoteric magic brought about by compound expansion but simply that the four cylinders had, in true Gallic style, been arranged in an elegant manner. Indeed, as a visit to the superb collection of French locomotives at Mullhouse will show, the French compound locomotives all possess that special quality of balance.

No 40 was built as an Atlantic for rough comparison with the French machines, but all subsequent 'Stars' were 4-6-0s, and *North Star* was soon converted to this form. The de Glehn compounds remained, they were sufficiently useful to warrant re-boilering, and they lasted until the end of the 1950s and probably went largely because their non-standard components needed replacing. Since two de Glehns are preserved near their birthplace one need not regret that these fine machines went to the scrapheap.

At this point, let Churchward speak for himself. In a letter dated 25 October 1909, to A.V. Goodyear, he deals with the question of cylinder proportions. The relevant paragraphs are:

"As you say, the 30 in stroke is not a disadvantage as commonly supposed. We have never noticed any abnormal wear and tear with the cylinders and pistons.

"It is correct that there are great advantages in the 30 in stroke in the matter of expansive working. The long stroke in relation to the bore is the only way we know of making the simple engine equal in efficiency to the compound engine.

"You are correct in assuming that the adoption of the 4-cylinder design was not on account of any dissatisfaction with the 18 in by 30 in cylinders – the relation of stroke to bore is even greater in the four cylinders than in the two cylinders. The four-cylinder engines are naturally better balanced and have their working parts very much lighter, so making them more suitable for high-speed expresses than would any two-cylinder engines of equivalent power.

"Yours truly

G.J. Churchward"

It is clear that with the four-cylinder layout Churchward not only achieved comparable efficiencies to the best current compound locomotives, but also produced a machine which could develop his desired two ton drawbar pull at 70 mph (112.6 km/h) with smooth ease. The 'Stars' did not supersede the simpler two-cylinder 'Saints', rather they were provided to work the fastest, heaviest trains. With the addition of a medium superheat, they proved more than capable of performing any required duty on the GWR.

It is therefore surprising that in 1908 an even larger machine was produced, the first British Pacific, No 111, *The Great Bear*. If any

enthusiast dreamed of a 'Constellation' class, he was to be disappointed. The GWR built no more Pacifics.

There is little doubt that No 111 was authorised as a publicity stunt; without doubt it settled who owned the largest passenger locomotive in Britain. Unfortunately, in every other respect it fell well short of the 'Stars'. Its weight and length effectively confined it to the London-Bristol line, and on that route, there was absolutely nothing that a 'Saint' could not romp away with. The big boiler was one of Swindon's rare flops; it steamed well, but not well enough. Finally, the rear axle gave trouble. The obvious solution, to replace it with one of the redundant sets of successful outside-framed axleboxes from the former Atlantics was not adopted, and it remains something of a mystery why this was not done. The probability is that the troubles were less than legend would have it, and it was not felt worth the expense in view of the small value of the locomotive. So in 1924, when the original boiler was past repair, the machine was rebuilt into a 'Castle'.

It is now known that a scheme was prepared to reconstruct the locomotive, with a modified version of the successful No 7 boiler and outside bearings to the

trailing axle. However, the opinion was that there was something about Pacifics that didn't suit Wiltshire, or vice versa. This was to have far reaching results.

Churchward foresaw that the time would come when the 'Stars' would be outclassed by increased traffic. Work began on the 'Super Star' project, marrying a larger boiler to the successful chassis. A new boiler, the No 7, was developed for the 47XX series of large 2-8-0s, and there was a general feeling that this, on a 'Star' chassis would meet the bill.

Unfortunately, not only did the resulting locomotive work out too heavy, but to clear the 6 ft 9½ in (2.05 m) drivers, the boiler needed to be pitched too high to suit the loading gauge. So it was back to the drawing board, and the result was a superb boiler, the No 8. Married to a slightly modified 'Star' chassis with a longer rear overhang and a more commodious side-window cab, the result was the 'Castle'.

It has often been suggested that the 'Castles' were a compromise. This is not so, they were the final version of the 'Super Star'. One has only to realise that not only was the chassis precisely that predicted, but the boiler pressure was identical. That the No 8 boiler

A Great Western Star of 1910, No 4035 *Queen Charlotte* with red/brown coaching stock.

was different in outline is immaterial. In the 'Castle', Swindon produced one of the finest steam locomotives ever built, it was powerful and extremely efficient. When in 1924 Collett released the test figures there was almost complete disbelief. This, more than the well known publicity stunt at Wembley, led to the locomotive interchanges of 1925 and to the development of the Gresley A3 'Super Pacific', since the trials clearly demonstrated that, regardless of nominal tractive effort, the advantages of high pressure and long travel valves could not be disputed.

Unfortunately, the use of tractive effort as a yardstick of performance became a habit, and when the Southern produced the 'Lord Nelson' class, with a higher tractive effort still, popular opinion began to hold that the GWR, long the exponents of big locomotives, had at last been outclassed. At about the same time, instead of reconstructing *The Great Bear* with a modified No 7 boiler and outside bearings on the trailing axle, a possibility that was explored, Collett rebuilt the machine into a 'Castle'. It was a sensible move, the 'Castles' were excellent machines and in place of an odd, almost useless engine, the company got a thoroughly useful machine. It was a fairly straightforward job; the main frames were cut between the second and third driving axles, and new extensions welded on. The provision of a No 8 boiler and a Collett cab completed the conversion. A normal 4,000 gallon (18,184 litre) tender was added, the bogie monstrosity went the rounds of lesser classes.

It has often been said that the 'Kings' originated because the Board and the General Manager were aghast to discover that the company had lost two distinctions. However, it is highly unlikely that the rebuild of *The Great Bear* was carried out without the knowledge

'The Cornish Riviera Limited' in its last year of steam working, hauled by No 6017 *King Edward IV*, entering Plymouth in 1957.

of the General Manager, or that he could not have mentioned it to the Board. Felix Pole's reminiscences are quite revealing, but they should be treated with some reservation since he was writing memoirs rather than a deeply-researched history, and there are obvious inconsistencies in his story.

Pole recalled that Sir Aubrey Brocklebank, a company director with a strong interest in locomotives, believed the 'Castles' were deficient. He also related that Collett admitted that, with an increase from the 19½ ton (19,305 kg) axle load limit then in force to 22 tons (22,353 kg), he could build a very fine locomotive. At the time, it seemed impossible.

Pole then went on to discuss the discovery that for some 22 years it had been the practice to renew all main line bridges to carry an axle load of 22 tons (22,353 kg), but that no one had seen fit in later years to inform the locomotive department of the fact. As a result, he was able to inform Collett that he could plan for a 22½ ton (22,861 kg) axle load for a four-cylinder machine, since

later experience had shown that most of the damage was caused not by deadweight, but by the hammerblow given by unbalanced reciprocating masses.

It is of interest that he makes no mention of greater tractive effort. In fact it is only introduced as something of an after-thought, as we shall see. The underlying reason for the production of the 'Kings' seems to have been the belief by Sir Aubrey Brocklebank, the one technically-minded member of the Board, that the 'Castles' were not quite the locomotive *he* wanted, coupled with the fact that loadings, particularly on the prestigious 'Cornish Riviera' express, were increasing to the point where 'Castles' were getting close to their practical limits. It is also clear that Collett wanted to build a bigger locomotive; but any CME who was not anxious to make bigger and better locomotives was clearly unfit for the job.

Details of the Design

Probably the most significant factor of the 'King' design was the fact that Felix Pole wanted the new locomotives in service for the summer of 1926. This does not indicate any great failings on the part of the 'Castles', for Pole was easily the most publicity-conscious General Manager any railway possessed. He first made his mark with the *GWR Magazine* which he transformed from a stolid staff journal into a lively, informative, if not always entirely accurate, journal which from about 1904 onwards carefully publicised the railway and proved conclusively that everything on the Great Western was automatically best. No doubt he was keenly interested in having for publicity purposes 'The Most Powerful Express Locomotive in Britain', but in fact he wanted a machine that would be needed for growing traffic, and was rather pleased that he had an influential ally on the Board of a like mind. It is important to remember that in 1926 everything looked good for the future of the railways. The General Strike had been broken and although the miners were still holding out it was clear they would be forced to accept the cuts. Business was booming and no one seriously considered the possibility of a slump, let alone the Great Depression.

It is probable that Collett had some ideas on the subject of a bigger locomotive, for although he has been put forward as a workshop man rather than a designer, he was a good all round engineer. Even if he had had no clear ideas on the subject, F.W. Hawkesworth, then in charge of the drawing office, certainly did.

The new locomotive was to be a 'Super Castle', however, many of the Churchward details were to be abandoned. The first to go was the driving wheel diameter. K.J. Cook has told us how Collett was travelling from Swindon to Paddington in an express when they were temporarily overtaken by a 43XX class mogul with 5 ft 8½ in (174 cm) diameter drivers on the relief line. Although Running Superintendent C.C. Crump, who was travelling with him, took the locomotive's number and was going to reprimand the driver, Collett stopped him, saying that he was very pleased to see it.

He accordingly gave orders that a 'Castle' was to be tried with the tyres turned down to 6 ft 6 in (1.98 m) diameter in place of the usual 6 ft 8½ in (2.04 m) diameter when new. Although this was below the wear limit, it was safe enough. Cook has pointed out that a new tyre would not have been subjected to the hammering that a worn tyre had received, and would therefore be tight. More probably, two other factors were of greater importance, the first being that the tyre allowance was set at a conservative figure. The second, and more cogent was that the locomotive was going to be carefully watched for the duration of the trials, and had the tyres shown any signs of weakness, those trials would have been aborted on the spot.

The locomotive so modified, according to Cook, was No 5002, *Ludlow Castle* but his account is wrong in one respect; he states this was done after a general repair, but No 5005 was only put into service in July 1926, and so it is clear the alteration was done as the locomotive went through its assembly.

The change in wheel diameter was an early decision. It ties in with Collett's previous decision to fit a 6 ft (1.82 m) diameter driver to a 'Saint', thus producing the 'Hall', rather than the 5 ft 8½ in (1.73 m) diameter predicted in the Churchward plan. No doubt at the outset the idea of boosting the tractive effort was considered, but the change in wheel diameter was more influenced by the need to use a larger diameter boiler than could be fitted above the 6 ft 8½ in (2.04 m) drivers.

An equally important divergence lay in the wheelbase. It was not merely the cylinders, wheels and motion that were common to Churchward designs, the spaces between the wheels were also standardised, and 7 ft (2.13 m) + 7 ft 6 in (2.3 m) was the rule of the day. The 'Kings' were spaced at 8 ft (2.44 m) + 8 ft 3 in (2.52 m). This has given rise to the idea that the 'King' ought to have been a Pacific.

There is, of course, no reason why the GWR should not have brought out a Pacific in 1927. The previous one admittedly had been something of a white elephant and there was a degree of prejudice concerning the whole concept. Churchward certainly seemed lukewarm about the idea and retired or not he still made a point of dropping into the works and making his views known. However, although it is possible to rebuild a 4-mm scale 'King' into a 4-6-2, by setting the drivers at 7 ft (2.13 m) + 7 ft (2.13 m) spacing, this brings the trailing axle immediately beneath the firebars. You can get away with this on an electrically-powered model, but on a full-sized steam locomotive, it is impossible. The long wheelbase of the 'King' was designed to suit the No 9 boiler, a very big affair, with the highest working pressure so far used on the GWR, 250 psi. It naturally possessed a larger grate, and as can be seen from the official diagram this dictated the spacing of the rear wheels, which in turn led to the proportional increase in the distance between the leading and centre drivers. Indeed, the 'King' chassis had to be extended mainly to accommodate the massive boiler.

The standard GWR four-cylinder

layout was followed. This was derived from the de Glehn arrangement, with the outside cylinders driving the centre coupled axle, the inside pair driving on the leading axle. Both sets of cylinders were horizontal, with each adjacent pair being diametrically opposed.

There was not complete reciprocating balance, this would require that all cylinders should drive on to a common axle. This particular arrangement would have permitted the use of a pair of castings, as with the two-cylinder types, but there has always been the idea that this could pose problems when the full power was exerted on a single pair of axleboxes, which on a standard gauge machine must be limited in width. Certainly the LNWR 'Claughtons' with this arrangement seemed to experience axlebox trouble, but this design was troublesome in other respects.

The valves were placed above and slightly to one side of the cylinders; they were even larger in diameter than on any previous GWR four-cylinder locomotive, and were driven by two sets of Walschaerts valve gear placed inside the frames driving both inside and outside valves through a set of rocker arms. The inside location of the valve gear has often been criticised, for Walschaerts gear is normally arranged outside, taking its drive from a return crank. This arrangement makes it accessible.

There is no doubt that the internal economy of a GWR four-cylinder locomotive was decidedly cramped, but no more so than any normal British inside-cylinder locomotive. The point is that apart from the need to see to the lubrication – and provision was made for this – it is not generally necessary to attend to valve gear. On the other hand, big ends, which had to transmit either half or a quarter of a locomotive's power output did require occasional

attention, and it was claimed that the GWR arrangement allowed the big ends to be taken down without having to dismantle the valve gear. Since this could mean resetting the valves, this was a consideration, but in practice it did not seem to be a problem. There is also the question of appearance, but again this is debatable. No one has ever suggested that Walschaerts valve gear in any way mars the appearance of a steam locomotive.

There is little doubt that originally the internal arrangement was dictated by the initial crosshead-driven 'scissors' gear of No 40, but this being the case, it is very significant that both valves are driven from the 'cold' end. If outside gear had been chosen then the inside valves would have been a little more tricky to set, since the expansion of the valve rod would upset the cold settings.

But it is not impossible to overcome this; it is irrelevant to argue that valves cannot be set accurately. Nevertheless, it is known that on the LNER, where conjugated gear was driven from the hot end, problems arose and serious consideration was given to arranging the gear on the cold side of the block, even at the cost of further complications.

The cylinders were enlarged to 16 in (40.6 cm) bore and 28 in (71.1 cm) stroke. This led to clearance troubles with the bogie. This problem was handed to one of the senior draughtsmen, A.W.J. Dymond, who decided that the most practical solution was to have the framing inside the rear pair of wheels and outside the front pair. He took his proposals to Collett, who approved them on the spot, which suggests that either Collett had seen the problem for himself and arrived at the same conclusion, or that Dymond put his proposals over with complete clarity, for novel designs normally require a long debate.

In retrospect it is a pity that the design was not scrutinised, for the wheel suspension was very

unsatisfactory and on 10 August 1927, No 6003, *King George IV*, not the steadiest of our monarchs, suffered a partial derailment near Midgham. Fortunately this happened on plain track, which made it clear that it was the locomotive which was at fault and the driver was able to stop the train without any further difficulties arising. It is said that Collett prodded the sleepers with his umbrella and tried to suggest that the track was at fault, but this is certainly just another Swindon myth. Immediate action was taken; in particular W.A. Stanier, who was with *King George V* in the USA was warned not to run at speed until the problem was resolved. The long-term solution was to modify the bogie springs and to add coil springs to the suspension roads. Certainly the initial arrangement appears extremely flimsy, although in practice it differed little from the highly successful arrangement employed on the outside framed bogies of the Dean era – and they held the track well enough.

Another modification that occurred early in the life of the class concerned the trailing axleboxes. Initially these had limited sideplay with Cartazzi pattern slide control, coupled with spherical bushes on the trailing coupling rods. Initial rough riding that occurred after several thousand miles was blamed on this feature, and so the boxes were changed for plain pattern slides, with no side play. The design inertia in the works was such that it was to be the 1950s before it occurred to anyone in authority that the spherical bushes were no longer necessary.

To complement the new design, a completely new tender was provided. This was not before time, since the standard 3,500 gallon pattern looked insignificant against a 'Star' and faintly ridiculous behind a 'Castle'. The new high-sided tender had a 4,000 gallon (18,184 litre) capacity and

Above: In April 1960 *King George V*, No 6000, takes the Cumbrian Coast Express on the first leg of its run to Wolverhampton.
Right: King George V, No 6000, as fitted with double chimney in 1950.

the coal plates were carried back to provide a deep box around the tank filler and pick-up dome. Although substantially similar tenders were fitted to the 'Castles' and 'Halls', the 'King' tenders formed a separate sub-class with larger water-pipe fittings, and were thus confined to the original locomotives.

The design, as prepared, had a nominal tractive effort of a fraction under 40,000 lbs (18,144 kg). When Collett showed the plans to Pole, he asked if the figure could be boosted, and Collett said it could. In his memoirs, Pole says it was done by taking ¼ in (0.5 cm) off the driving wheel diameter. He was mistaken, the cylinders were bored out an additional ¼ in (0.5 cm) and this was sufficient to bring the nominal tractive effort to the quoted 40,300 lbs (18,280 kg). Collett had ordered a rebore, taking up much of the wear allowance on the cylinders. He did not redesign the cylinders and furthermore after the initial batch of six were completed the locomotives came out of works with 16 in (40.6 cm) diameter cylinders as new.

This brings home several points about tractive effort. The first is that, although confidently bandied about as an absolute standard, it is appreciably affected by the normal intermediate repairs on the locomotive; not only can the cylinders be bored out by slightly more than the ¼ in (0.5 cm) of the initial 'Kings', but the diameter of the driving wheels is progressively reduced as the tyres are turned. The boiler pressure also has a very significant bearing, and although TE is calculated at a reduced percentage, it can be modified by the simple practice of upping the percentage.

A side issue brought out by Pole's story is the relative difficulty of calculating tractive effort before the advent of pocket calculators. The formula is not complicated but there are enough steps to make it tedious. It is certain that Collett

was well aware that opening up the cylinder bore by a small margin would do the trick. What he couldn't do was an on the spot check since a slide rule, the only calculator he was likely to have had, will only give three figure accuracy at best. A slide rule is not known as a guessing stick for nothing, it can tell roughly whether a particular line is worth exploring in detail, but for accuracy, designers in the years BC (before calculators), relied on tables and seven-figure logarithms, or in some cases, straightforward long division and multiplication. It is unlikely that any commentator ever bothered to work out the figures for the 'King', for a couple of minutes with a calculator shows that the well-known story only lines up with a cylinder enlargement.

It is worth emphasising again that Felix Pole's reminiscences were privately published, and intended solely for family and friends, he was not writing a definitive account for the histories. He made copies available to several leading writers, who drew upon them, and in 1968 a reprint was issued.

He makes no mention in the book of a matter which it is said he raised with the well-known model engineer, Jimmy Crebbin, that the increase in tractive effort on the 'Kings' led to a considerable cost in patterns, tools and machinery. That there were extra costs for patterns was inevitable and some new tools, principally flanging blocks, were required. However, it is difficult to assess exactly what new machinery was required, since the existing wheel lathes were perfectly suitable, indeed, it is likely that the one needed for the 7 ft 8 in (2.34 m) singles had not been scrapped by the mid 1920s. The boring machines could cope with the cylinders with ease, they could tackle the larger two-cylinder types. We are therefore left with a lingering suspicion that either Jimmy Crebbin misunderstood

Pole or that Collett had taken the opportunity of the new design to order some additional plant which would replace some of the older machine tools. This is a standard engineering practice and Collett, by all accounts very much a workshop man, would take any opportunity to improve the already high standards of the Swindon factory.

It has often been said that originally the class was to be called 'Cathedrals' and that the decision to name them after 'Kings' was only taken when it was decided to send the prototype to the USA. Cook states that this is not so and, as Assistant to the Works Manager, he was very much concerned with the construction of the class and took particular interest in names and numbers. He goes on to say that the story probably originated in a spoof article in the *Swindon Advertiser*, that in turn probably originated in the general and building side of the drawing office.

The 'Kings' were named in reverse chronological order, beginning with the current reigning monarch. This meant that the sub-group of 'Stars' bearing King names had to be re-named. They received a rather ungainly 'Monarch' title and in World War II were duly censored as various countries became enemies. At the same time, two of the small double-framed 4-4-0s lost their names – 'Bulldog' class to No 3361, *Edward VII* and 'Duke' class No 3257 *King Arthur*. There seems no reason for the last of the deletions, but there was a fit of nameplate removal at the time when all the town names were removed lest passengers confused them with destination boards.

Above: King George III No 6004 brings the up Birkenhead express into Snow Hill. Birmingham in October 1956.

Below: Down 'Torbay Express' in October 1934 with spotless carriages hauled by King No 6018 *King Henry VI* with red headlamps.

Above: In August 1962 *King Richard III*
No 6015 enters Shrewsbury with down
Cambrian Coast Express past the former
LNWR signal box.

Below: A clean *King Henry V* No 6019 hauls
an up extra past Kingskerswell in April 1962.

The last days of the Great Western. *King Charles I* No 6010 in GWR livery in April 1947 near Reading.

Below: King George V No 6000 in BR blue with Hungry Lion logo ex works passing Chippenham, running-in – July 1949.

Left: King George VI No 6028 with the up 'Capitals Express' near Wootton Bassett in September 1960.
Below: The 11.00 am Birmingham to Paddington near Seer Green in September 1962 hauled by *King Henry VIII* No 6013.

Right: No 6029 *King Edward VIII* on a down Plymouth excursion at Tigley Box in September 1960.

Left, above: Picking up water on Goring troughs No 6019 *King Henry V* with double chimney heads the 'Red Dragon' in March 1961.

Above: A preserved *King George V* in October 1973 near Church Stretton on the 'Atlantic Venturers Express'.

In high summer 1957 *King Charles II* leaves Dawlish with the 13.25 Paddington to Kingswear.

Above: 'The Zenith' Special in November 1980 leaving Shrewsbury for Chester with steam surround.

Below: King George V No 6000 in September 1979 with Restaurant Car Special near Little Stretton.

Above: The control end of No 6017, *King Edward IV*, at Swindon in October 1957.

Below: King Edward I at Wolverhampton in June 1961.

Above left: No 6029, *King Edward VII*, in British Rail livery at Wolverhampton in June 1961 with breakdown crane in background.
Above right: King Edward IV empties its cylinders of water preparing to depart with an up train from Wolverhampton in April 1962.
Below: King Edward VI, No 6017, at Swindon in April 1960, prior to overhaul.

The Fair of the Iron Horse

If any of those present at the formal opening of the Baltimore & Ohio Railroad in 1827 had been told that they were to force a British locomotive works to accelerate the completion of a new locomotive a century later, they would almost certainly have laughed. Yet this is precisely what happened.

In the 1920s the President of the B&O decided to celebrate his railroad's centenary and, as the British were making something of the 1825 opening of the Stockton & Darlington, he commissioned Ed Hungerford to go and see how the Limeys were setting about it. Hungerford met Felix Pole during the celebrations and Pole sold him the idea that there should not only be a British locomotive at the celebrations, but that it must be a Great Western locomotive, and in due course the invitation was extended.

In the interim, the new locomotive class was being produced, and to Pole there could be no question of sending an outmoded 'Castle', it had to be one of the new machines. Moreover, it had to work and work well.

Everything was going well at the works, the first locomotive was due to leave the factory in September 1927. Apparently, Pole's directive that the new locomotives had to be ready for service in the summer of 1927 had not been passed on to the production team. Cook, then assistant to the works manager, has told how his Chief, R.A.G. Hannington, asked him to come and see Collett's deputy, W.A. Stanier. When Cook explained that the first locomotive was due out in September, he was bluntly told,

"Young man, she's got to be in the USA by August." This was December 1926, and at the time very few drawings had been issued, and the only work in any way advanced was the production of the boiler flanging blocks. No doubt the drawing office received a similar sharp reminder!

It is on record that No 6000, *King George V,* entered service the following June, and the next five, those with oversize cylinders, followed in July. *King George V* was fitted with Westinghouse brake gear for operation in the USA, and, so fitted, set out on its maiden journey at the head of the 'Cornish Riviera' express on 20 July, a heavily retouched photograph of the start appearing as the frontispiece of the *Great Western Railway Magazine* for September 1927. By then, *King George V* had made its US visit and this same issue records the departure of the locomotive, accompanied by the reconstructed 'North Star', on 3 August.

The locomotive was shipped from Cardiff. Unlike Liverpool or Glasgow, where export of locomotives was part and parcel of the business of the port, Cardiff was in the main concerned with coal, and the largest crane could only manage a lift of 70 tons (71,124.5 kg), and so for the trip it was necessary to separate boiler from chassis, and to mount the two as separate items of deck cargo on the SS *Chicago City*, a remarkably small vessel of the Bristol City Line, 285 ft (86.9 m) between perpendiculars and only 1,478 registered tonnage; even for the 1920s, this was a rather odd choice, unless there was some element of patronage.

The crossing was eventful, the vessel ran into typical Western Ocean weather and the motion became more than a little lively. Captain C.B. Short, then First Officer of the *Chicago City* and a thoroughly experienced seaman, had seen to the securing of the load, but there had been some

Looking as a locomotive should, *King George V* arrives at Stratford-upon-Avon with an appropriately named train in 1983.

problems. For example, the load was such that part of the standing rigging had had to be unshipped to allow the locomotive to be loaded and the deck strengthened by shoring from beneath. The locomotive had been immaculately finished, and had to arrive at Baltimore in a like condition, which meant that every lashing had to be carefully seized to prevent it chafing. Short had introduced shores, and had found what he thought was a perfect location, under the footplate above the driving wheels. He put on record that he had no idea that he'd picked the wrong place until he saw for himself at 3 am, in heavy weather, the chassis dancing up and down on its springs, and his shores floating about in the water on the deck. Fortunately, the lashings were tight and the load was secure, but one shudders to think what could have happened had Short and his men not made a very good job of securing the locomotive in Cardiff.

At Baltimore the locomotive was unloaded and reassembled. This was no great problem, for not only were GWR boilers designed to come on and off easily, but the then Assistant CME, Stanier, was there to supervise the work of chargeman Fred Williams and fitter George Dando, who had gone on ahead on another ship together with crates of spares.

There is no doubt that everyone had gone to tremendous pains to ensure that *King George V* was in perfect condition and although there is no record of anything unusual being done, it would be highly unlikely that anything short of absolute perfection of finish was permitted. Everything that could be polished was polished and the paintwork was immaculate. Combined with the clean, uncluttered line of the design, this

King George V on its way to Stratford, passing Aynho with a train full of enthusiasts.

'The William Shakespeare', No 6000 *King George V*, en route from Didcot to Stratford.

was a complete contrast with US locomotive practice, where no one thought it worthwhile spending anything on frills. The comparatively silent running added to the effect.

Without doubt driver Young, ably supported by fireman Pearce, the team who had been so effective in the 1925 locomotive trials, should get much of the credit, for although the hard-working standard US two-cylinder locomotive was a noisy beast, a 'King' was by no means silent, as anyone can check from the many recordings currently available. However, a clever driver can reduce the noise by easing up a little when he spots a spectator. Driver Young went one better; noticing that there was a small downgrade immediately before the grandstand on the parade ground, he all but shut off steam. As *King George V* had been given the premier position in the procession, he could get away with this, and the contrast with the clanking locomotives that pushed him along was extremely noticeable.

There was one slight worry; as recounted in the previous chapter, whilst *King George V* was on the high seas No 6003, *King George IV*, derailed at Midgham, casting doubts on the running qualities of the leading bogie. Stanier was informed in strict confidence and until some suggestions for adjusting the weight on the bogie were sent, *King George V* was only run at moderate speeds. Fortunately, there was no reason for the hosts to expect the British visitors to prove anything before the show, and by the time a demonstration run was due, the bogie was passed as satisfactory. Some comment has been made on the poorer quality of US track, but this was sheer prejudice. Some western railroads did have low-grade trackage, but the major lines maintained their main routes as well as any European line, and it would be wrong to imply that the Baltimore & Ohio's main line was

in any way suspect.

The demonstration run on 17 October was not in any way a record-breaking event, just a good stiff run with seven heavyweight B & O cars behind, a somewhat heavier load than the 'Cornish Riviera'. *King George V* acquitted itself well, and returned covered in glory. Without doubt, great credit must go to fireman Pearce, who had to contend with a completely different grade of coal than usual. However, he succeeded so well that he maintained a reasonable pressure throughout and kept the exhaust so clean that many American locomotive engineers were convinced that the design of the firebox was something out of the ordinary. The heavy smoke associated with US locomotive running was more the result of a less stringent outlook in general. Not only were fewer US lines surrounded by houses, but few railroads went anywhere near the homes of any but the poorest in the community, most of whom had long since given up complaining about anything.

During the show *King George V*

was attended by the complete contingent, prepared to explain to the former colonists exactly how superior their locomotive was. There is no doubt that many people were impressed, even Henry Ford was moved to take some photographs and announced that he intended to build a model. Whether he actually did is not recorded, and whilst he was by no means the first model-maker to be inspired by the 'Kings' he remains the best-known. One hopes that Paddington sent him a set of drawings in return for the free publicity he provided.

The locomotive was also graced by a young lady dressed as Britannia. O.S. Nock states she was Miss Lillian Schuler, daughter of one of the Directors of the B & O. However, the *GWR Magazine* for December 1927, refers to her as Miss Bruhl in the caption to a photograph in which she appears with W.A. Stanier and the loco crew and mechanics. As the

No 6017, *King Edward VI*, takes the up 'Cornish Riviera' through Hemerden Bank in 1951 in early BR livery with a mixed collection of coaches.

accompanying notes are by Stanier who probably captioned the photo, it is more than likely that although on the opening day Miss Schuler took the limelight, for the rest of the show Miss Bruhl did the work.

There were many encomiums from the various people concerned, but no more than one would expect under the circumstances. The report on the trial run only specifically mentioned the smooth riding but also mentioned driver Young's work, which obviously impressed the test engineers as much as did the locomotive. There was some slight effect on US loco design, a couple of machines were tidied up, but this was a temporary aberration. One individual seeing

King Edward VI No 6012, taking the up 11.00 from Birmingham, near Beaconsfield in April 1962.

the locomotive at work was moved to say, "Boy, that's not a locomotive, that's a clock!" In view of his comment on seeing the French compounds from which the design evolved, Churchward would have been delighted, but so far as can be ascertained Captain Short, who recorded the incident, did not mention this until long after the Chief had gone to rest.

The return was not without incident, for when the locomotive was due to be loaded back on the *Chicago City,* the entire crew of the only floating crane powerful enough to lift the locomotive were in jail. It was a family-run crane, father and sons; the charge was drunkenness. In the best traditions of Hollywood B movies, they were bailed to allow them to load the locomotive in time.

The locomotive returned with some extra fittings. There was an

engraved commemorative bell, which read:

PRESENTED TO THE LOCOMOTIVE KING GEORGE BY THE BALTIMORE AND OHIO RAILROAD IN COMMEMORATION OF ITS CENTENARY CELEBRATIONS SEPT 24 – OCT 15 1927

and a commemorative medal. Copies of the medal were cast and fixed to the cabside. The medal itself was occasionally carried inside the cab until an unscrupulous souvenir hunter made off with it. The GWR made much of these courtesies, even implying that the medal was a mark of merit. In fact the publicity gained from this visit more than outweighed the cost, and it was no more than a minor incident in the USA, where few enthusiasts even knew that a British locomotive was at the Fair.

The First Kings in Service

If *King George V* did not shine as brightly in the USA as the Paddington publicity machine suggested, the other five early locomotives were proving their worth on their home metals. This needs to be emphasised.

The 'Kings' marked a break with Churchward principles in many respects. The basic design was enlarged, the hitherto sacrosanct 7 ft (2.1 m) + 7 ft 9 in (2.36 m) coupled wheelbase abandoned, the driving wheels were reduced in diameter, and a completely new boiler was introduced. The design, although following the principles laid down in 1904, was not a 'Super Star'. Yet whereas each new Churchward design was preceded by a prototype, which underwent evaluation before the main class was put into production, twenty 'Kings' were ordered off the drawing board under Lot 243 and, apart from a small modification to the completely novel leading bogie, remained substantially unaltered for nearly a quarter of a century thereafter, whilst performing the most arduous duties on the line with complete reliability.

Furthermore, this was no carefully nurtured design taken through the various stages of development with deliberate, careful precision. It was conceived and built in a hurry with the General Manager personally urging haste. When the LMS was pushed into ordering the 'Royal Scots', much has been made of the fact that the locomotives came out right at the beginning, yet an almost identical situation on the GWR has been taken for granted for the best part of half a century.

It is true that the situation on the GWR was in no way similar, for the operating department had the 'Stars', the 'Saints' and over thirty 'Castles' for top rank duties. Nevertheless the untried 'Kings' went into service with all the attendant fuss of an overheated publicity machine, a process calculated to draw attention to any defects.

No 6000, *King George V,* took the 'Cornish Riviera' out of Paddington on 20 July 1927, non-stop to Plymouth after it had run its normal running in turns. The load was moderate, it was a Wednesday, the load was only 425 tons (431,827 kg) to Westbury and 350 tons (355,622 kg) beyond. However, this was the first time such a large, unassisted load was taken over the South Devon banks; tare for the class was fixed at 360 tons (365,783 kg).

On paper at least. Two days later No 6001, *King Edward VII,* took a load of 375 tons tare (381,024 kg) over the banks and with a crowded train it approached 400 tons (406,425 kg) full. In the winter timetables, seven minutes were cut off the schedule of the train.

At this point the publicity recoiled. Despite their size and massive tractive effort, there didn't seem much to show for it. After all, if one took the best performances of the 'Stars' or the 'Castles' it was quite possible that similar savings in time could have been made without going to the trouble and expense of building a new locomotive.

It is perhaps as well to emphasise one important point that locomotive students often overlook. The public view any transport organisation differently. They look at the published timetables and ask themselves "can I believe it?". In the 1920s, public confidence had been sapped by the aftermath of the coal strike, and although the GWR had gone a long way towards restoring this confidence, it was a fragile thing. It was far more important to run from Paddington to Plymouth North Road in the promised time than it was to put up a fast run four days out of six, but to arrive late on the other two – especially if the two in question happened to be over the busy weekend. The fact is that a responsible railway publishes timetables which they believe are factual, that if they promise a non-stop run from London to Plymouth of 240 minutes, they achieve it. How they achieve it is another matter.

This was fully demonstrated in October when Cecil J. Allen was invited to travel on the footplate. The load was moderate, 525 tons (533,433 kg) out of Paddington, successively reduced by slipping until only 270 tons (274,337 kg) remained for the stiffest part of the journey. The locomotive was No 6005, *King George II,* whose main distinction was that he was the least distinguished of all the Hanoverians. This was an augury, for Murphy's Law was about to strike; the tender was loaded with indifferent coal. The result was that time was lost on the first part of the journey, but the crew worked valiantly and although they were six minutes behind schedule at Savernake, they had regained four minutes by the time they reached Taunton. At Exeter the train was three minutes behind time, but with the load reduced Plymouth was reached ahead of time. Cecil Allen, being an LNER employee, loyally made the most of the opportunity. But it was suggested that, in enlarging the Churchward concept, a serious mistake had been made by not adopting a wide firebox. Questions were asked in enthusiast circles and remained unanswered.

The following year, Allen was given another run, this time on the footplate of No 6011, *King James I.* With top quality coal, the actual performance of the locomotive was far superior, and he said so. Indeed, he was impressed by the fact that although the run was

The return to Paddington. *King George V* leaves on its first run from the station in years, accompanied by one of the anonymous, but still highly regarded, HST sets.

marred by no less than eight permanent way slacks, the 'net' timing was only 228 minutes. Unfortunately, the actual time was just over 245 minutes, and although a railway enthusiast would understand the reason, the majority of the passengers must have been disappointed.

These two runs are a perfect example of how easy it is to allow technical knowledge to obscure reality. The object of a locomotive is to haul a train to the schedules laid down by the operating department, preferably at a profit. If, quite incidentally, it provides amusement because it is named, or because its particular behaviour at some chance moment happens to attract the favourable attention of one of a small group of specialised enthusiasts, so much the better. However, if it meets the last two criteria, but cannot keep to the organised schedules, then it is useless.

In 1928, as more and more top line crews became used to the 'Kings' and learned how to utilise the nominal tractive effort without running out of steam, the day-to-day performance of the class on the West of England run settled down, and the heaviest of loads were confidently run when needed. Full use was made of the extra potential of the big boiler, and even the more critical enthusiasts began to agree that the 'Kings' did have an edge over the highly successful 'Castles'. We must never forget that this was not a case of a new locomotive with a considerable advantage over what already existed, the 'Kings' had to compete with one of the finest designs of all time.

Typical of their work around this time was a run by No 6000, *King George V* on 7 July 1929. Starting with 14 coaches (479 tons (486,695 kg) tare), three were slipped at Westbury, reducing the load to 11 (378 tons (384,072 kg)). A steady start was made, and Southall was passed in 12 minutes, rather than 11 minutes as expected. This was just a case of the driver setting his own pace for by the time he reached Reading he was fractionally ahead of time, and despite a permanent way slack at Woodborough and signal checks on the approaches to Taunton, Exeter was passed just over one second ahead of schedule.

The tare load, 378 tons (384,072 kg), was over the limit, but the driver was completely confident, passing Newton Abbot some four minutes ahead of time. A little of this was lost climbing the bank, but at Brent the train was still fractionally ahead of time. The train had a clear run into Plymouth, and arrived three minutes ahead of time. The run was a clear demonstration that the driver had the load completely in hand, the locomotive was working well within its limits, and there was a margin for the occasional permanent way slack or signal check.

By the summer of 1928,

Right: June 1960, Western Region King Class No 6022 with the down Bristol express passing Castle Class No 5062.
Below: 'The Welsh Mountain Pullman' – No 6000 *King George V.*

sufficient 'Kings' were available to permit some to be drafted to the Birmingham route. The initial results were not good. The route is a taxing one with long stretches of fairly stiff adverse grades, and although these are balanced by equivalent downgrades, there is no doubt that the tight, competitive timings set locomotive men a formidable task.

Initially it seems that the Wolverhampton crews had some problems. The 'Kings' could run fast enough downhill, but despite their high nominal power they had problems maintaining schedules uphill; it was a simple matter of

mastering the machines, and in particular of the fireman learning how best to pace his firing. As Sam Ell was to demonstrate in the post-war years, the real limit of power output on the larger GWR locomotives was the fireman's ability to shovel coal into the firebox fast enough to keep up with the needs of the system.

Another point that becomes obvious from a careful analysis of the published logs from the period is that the 'Kings' were, for the most part, more than masters of their work, and in a way they were premature. There were few duties where a 'Castle' was so extended

that an indifferent crew, or poor fuel, could seriously affect the locomotive's ability to run the train to the schedules set down. There was no pressing commercial reason for making a dramatic cut in the timings of any one train, bearing in mind the knock-on effect of such a shift. One fact is important: in 1930, the *slower* GWR services to Plymouth were appreciably faster than any generally available alternative. Only a very experienced driver using a high-performance car of the period could outpace a train; the old A38, known as the longest lane in Britain, saw to that!

The 1930s

Quality control at its best. The finished product, No 6009 *King Charles II*.

The first six 'Kings' appeared by July 1927 and considerable pressure was exerted to get these into service for the Summer season. The balance of Lot 243 did not appear until the following year, No 6006 entering service in February and No 6019, the last of the batch, in July. On paper there were now 20 high-powered 4-6-0s available for the 1928 Summer services, for it seems highly unlikely that any of the first six had by then amassed sufficient mileage to require attention.

A further 10 were put into hand under Lot 267 and appeared between May and August 1930. No further 'Kings' were built.

In 1930, during the meeting called to consider the future programme, R.A.G. Hannington put forward the proposition that a further batch of 'Kings' should be put into hand. W.N. Pellow, who was standing in for the Locomotive Running Superintendent, pointed out that his department would prefer more 'Castles'. Collett immediately asked why they didn't want more of his 'Kings', and Pellow pointed out that the routes over which 'Kings' could work were limited in comparison with those available to 'Castles' and that they had enough 'Kings' anyway. He similarly opposed a move to produce more of the heavy 83XX series 2-6-0s in favour of the more useful 43XX versions.

Bearing in mind that, *at that time,* there were only 46 'Castles', including the 'Star' rebuilds, and that the next batch of locomotives were needed to allow more of the small 6 ft 8½ in (2.04 m) 4-4-0s to be replaced, Pellow's objections made sense. There were enough 'Kings' to work, not the traffic over the double red routes, but the traffic over those routes that was likely to stretch the more useful

'Castle' class, and that the need was for more four-cylinder machines on the services where 'Kings' were not essential, allowing 'Saints' and 'Stars' to be rostered to the less important trains.

In retrospect the decision was unfortunate, although it did avoid one problem. Whereas under Churchward, the principle of class names was applied in batches, under Collett and subsequently under Hawkesworth, it became far too rigid. In time, the 'Castles' exhibited some variations, but it was not until the war years that the new locomotives were named out of the class scheme. Other classes remained solidly monolithic, indeed. Not only were fears expressed that the supply of 'Halls' might dry up, but many facetious suggestions were put forward for further names.

The kings of England are limited in number, and with No 6029, *King Stephen,* they were getting perilously close to the point where it is open to debate whether earlier monarchs could be described as kings of England in the same way. Another twenty locomotives would have led to quite a few problems, particularly as the Anglo-Saxon dynasties were not only confused, but were obstinately unnumbered. One

immediately has to consider the case of No 6034, *King Edward the Confessor,* without trying to work out where Ethelred the Unready would fit. (And do you, or do you not, count the Norse usurpers?). A batch of 20 would have brought up the question of whether or not to list *King Arthur*, whilst Cymbeline (or Cunobelius, if you want to use the historic character) was more of a tribal chieftain than anything else. It is unlikely that this seriously affected the deliberations during that meeting. Few locomotive engineers are unduly bothered about names, but it could have had some slight bearing on the subject.

The unfortunate thing is that this consideration apparently did put a stop to serious thought of whether more 'Kings' could have been profitably employed. Even the most casual study of locomotive working reveals that there were plenty of trains working exclusively over double red routes which were habitually worked by 'Castles', and had either Lot 295 or Lot 296 (both for 10 'Castles'), been converted to 'Kings', further accelerations could have been considered. Even without this, another 10 'Kings' would have been a godsend on summer

Saturdays, where loadings on all West Country services were right up to the limit, and the time lost by the use of underpowered locomotives, or the need to double head beyond Newton Abbot, added considerably to the congestion on those lines. One major reason many holiday makers turned to the car was because of the uncertain arrival times on Saturdays. That they then experienced even greater delays on the Exeter by-pass was irrelevant.

The 'Kings' proved excellent locomotives, smooth-running and fast once the springing had been modified on the bogies and the trailing axlebox springs. It is a matter for regret that the GWR appeared to have lost interest in speed as such. There was the 'Cheltenham Flyer', officially the 'Cheltenham Spa Express', a relatively unimportant train which, because it was lightly loaded and ran at a time when a clear path could be arranged, showed what speeds were possible on Brunel's well-aligned main line and for a few glorious years was 'The Fastest Train in the World'. It was usually a 'Castle' run and underlined Paddington's disinterest in speed records.

There was a good reason for this lack of interest. One fast schedule in a bevy of mediocre services is little more than an irritant, not only to the travelling public but also to railway staff in general. It is far better to provide a good, all round service; here there is good cause for large numbers of fast locomotives, capable of maintaining tight schedules under normal day to day conditions. Throughout the 1930s, this was the objective of all the 'Big Four' but the GWR, thanks to the foresight shown in the first years of the century was best able to raise overall levels of service with a very large selection of fast 4-6-0s.

A contributory factor was the fact that the GWR could rely upon ample supplies of Welsh steam coal. This much is fully appreciated, but what is not always remembered is that the GWR adopted a radically different approach to coaling than did the northern lines. The GWR did not favour mechanical coaling plants but preferred the old fashioned raised stage instead.

To a certain extent, the friable nature of Welsh coal influenced this decision. A coaling plant involves dropping coal from a great height then shaking it about in a large bunker, producing a good deal of small coal in the process. Coal is a very variable fuel, and very little can be done to standardise the end product at reasonable cost. But it can be discovered how a particular seam will perform by practical experiment. Coal is bought direct at the pithead and loaded immediately into wagons; it is fairly simple to keep a note of what is good, and what is not so good. But when the whole load is tipped into a large bunker, it becomes a matter of pot luck what goes into the tender.

On the other hand, on a large manual stage with several chutes, it is relatively simple to sort the wagons so that certain chutes get the best coal, and that locomotives on the most arduous duties only get the very best. Needless to say, throughout the 1930s both 'Kings' and 'Castles' normally received top quality coal, and when the shed knew that the run was going to be taxing, the coal was liable to be hand picked.

Of course, there are numerous records of the performance of the 'Kings' in traffic. Unfortunately, the published logs largely reveal the artificial nature of the game, for the records are mainly aimed at assessing a performance figure which is as contrived as tractive effort. Furthermore, as the exponents of the art have pointed out, the actual passing time depends on the location of the observer in a train of anything from 10 to 14 coaches. Although the tare load can be readily estimated by walking along the train and noting the weight of the coaches, conveniently recorded on the ends, the actual load can never be more than an inspired guess. If it were possible to arrive at a meaningful assessment of locomotive performance by this method, railway companies would never have gone to the trouble of manufacturing dynamometer cars.

W.A. Tuplin has gone so far as to suggest that it is perfectly easy to produce a plausible log without bothering to note any passing time at all, which overlooks the fact that it is a pleasant way of occupying a journey. Unfortunately for the historian, the results have been traditionally presented in a wholly artificial fashion. We are given a load figure, very rarely the number of coaches and never their type. In place of actual time we have elapsed time and, where the journey involves a stop, no indication of the duration of that stop. Since the coach-borne observer has no way of knowing the boiler pressure, the cut-off percentage indicated, or any other relevant data, one is left with a rough assessment of locomotive performance but no indication of train running.

It is quite clear from the logs that the loads appeared to be set proportionate to the motive power and that 'Kings' were generally rostered to take the heaviest trains. The quoted loads correspond with 13 to 14 coaches and of course this is the practical limit of the main stations. This brings home a significant feature of railway operation; the real limitation on trains is set as much by the fixed structures as on the motive power itself. The logs suggest that arrivals were as near on time as to make no practical difference. An amusing sidelight is that wherever there were slacks on the run, the artificial 'net time' shows that the locomotives generally had a margin in hand which a keen crew

Above: Birmingham Railway Museum. *King George V* No 6000 in company with *Clun Castle*, No 7029, the last Castle to work out of Paddington, and LMS Contemporary – the Jubilee class *Kolhapur*.
Right: 'The Welsh Marches Express' pulled by No 6000 *King George V* heads south at Marshbrook en route from Shrewsbury to Hereford.

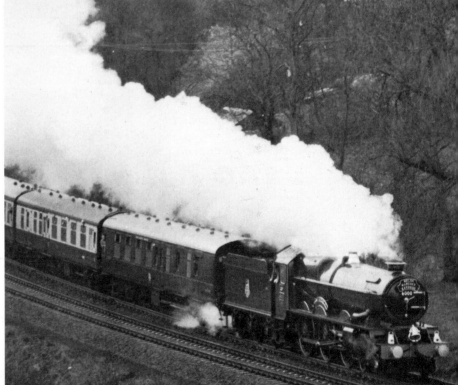

could exploit. In order to get a 'sparkling' performance it is necessary not only to have a good crew with a locomotive in good order, with decent coal and clean tubes, but a couple of hold-ups en route.

The importance of knowing the type of coaches, rather than their total deadweight has quite a bearing on the subject of performance. Coach weight is not the only significant factor, the rolling resistance has a considerable bearing. In the 1930s, the GWR made two important changes. The first was to abandon the longer 70 ft (21.3 m) coach in favour of shorter vehicles, generally around 60 ft (18.3 m) in length, which had fewer route restrictions. On longer trains, this could amount to an extra coach and four extra axles for roughly the same weight, a different thing altogether.

However, to a large extent this was set against the steady introduction of 'blue axlebox' stock. A new design of coach bearing was devised that offered lower friction and greater freedom from hot boxes and, in order that the operating staff could recognise the stock so fitted, without having to refer to a list of coach numbers, the new boxes were painted a very distinctive bright blue. As soon as sufficient blue axlebox stock was to hand, instructions went out that the most important trains were only to be run with blue axlebox coaches.

It is important to realise that the GWR did not own sufficient coaches to allow for every service to have fixed rakes allocated, with a sprinkling of coaches left around the system solely to strengthen the heaviest loadings. Instead, at the carriage sidings it was the practice to re-form sets to meet the demand. Old Oak Common, the main centre on the system, was particularly adept at this. Of course certain important named trains had a complete set of the latest coaches allocated to a specific

service and major trains were left more or less intact as far as possible. Similarly, the local shuttle services remained fixed, with either non-corridor stock or older main line coaches in the 1930s, corridor clerestory stock from the turn of the century.

Where a long-distance train was likely to wait for several hours at the far end of the line, part of it would be employed on a short local service; whilst at the main stations, coaches would be borrowed to strengthen an earlier service, then other stock would have to be moved around to replace those that had gone elsewhere. Although this juggling sounds haphazard, it was a very sophisticated operation, depending in the main on the knowledge and experience of the senior carriage shunters at each set of storage sidings. Intensive use of stock is not a new idea by any means!

A very important development that affected all GWR locomotives took place in 1934, when Swindon was equipped with Zeiss optical lining up equipment. On any machine, the precise alignment of bearings and other working surfaces is vital if free running and long life are required. There are various traditional methods of arranging this, but where the surfaces are separated by a matter of feet the traditional method was to use wires.

The method was simple enough on the face of it. Fine steel wires were stretched along the nominal centre line and the various parts set up from this datum. In practice it wasn't quite so simple. The wire would tend to take up a catenary curve rather than a straight line, and although this could be modified by placing it under tension, it placed considerable strain on the fixings and made fine adjustment of those fixings more difficult; and there was always the feeling that the wire could break, and the whiplash from 10 or 15 feet of wire under tension was

potentially dangerous. In addition, the wire was easily displaced accidentally whilst measurements were being taken. Finally, it was essential for locomotives to align the main bearings in two planes, at right angles to each other: along the frames to ensure that the cylinders were in line, and across the frames to ensure that the bearings were both parallel and, in the case of the driving axle, in line with the cylinders.

The Zeiss equipment used light in place of the wire, since for all practical purposes the implications of relativity could be ignored. The light beam has no mass and is perfectly straight. Of course, the principle of sighting is as old as technology; the difference here was the sophistication of the equipment, which not only permitted both axleboxes to be measured with reference to the centre line of the cylinders, but also the distance between horn guides could be measured with precision. Cook wrote an article in the November 1934 *GWR Magazine* which explained, in reasonably simple terms, the use of the equipment.

What he did not reveal at the time was that it was only part of the re-equipment of the works. Following the acquisition of the Zeiss Collimator, the GWR investigated two machines that would grind the horn cheeks *in situ*. Neither design was considered satisfactory, and a consultant, James Say, devised a version that could be used with the horn ties in position and, in its original form, with the motion bar brackets in place on certain classes. This device could be correctly set up with the Zeiss equipment, ensuring that within extremely fine limits the bearing guides were absolutely true. The new process was first used during the construction of a batch of 'Castles' under Lot 295, but it was also used on all major overhauls, and as the 'Kings' came in they too were set up optically.

Another device produced around this time was an improved crank-pin quartering gauge, an extremely sophisticated application of the common spirit level, and as with much other specialised equipment this was constructed entirely within the works.

The combination of these requirements led to smoother running and greater reliability. This was applied to all locomotives as they went through the works and whilst the improvements were marginal, it did mean that the majority of locomotives were sent out in the way the designers intended, and their reliability in service went up.

Another detail improvement lay in the actual bearings. Intensive study of failures and their causes led to small design changes and most important of all, radical alterations to the design of oil wells.

The most important change was the abolition of the traditional wick feed. Enginemen were a conservative group, convinced that they knew better than those clever chaps in the drawing office; they would certainly continue to use the worsted trimmings in spite of everything, so a restrictor plug was introduced into the feed tube. The term was something of a misnomer, for when the idea was

taken over to the LMS, careful tests were performed to show that the plug did not restrict the flow of oil at all. It had to be pointed out that its purpose was to restrict the use of worsted trimmings!

The improvement in lubrication was most important where 'Kings' were concerned, for this high power output placed considerable stress on the connecting rod big ends and there was a certain amount of trouble with the inside big ends. This particular trouble was not unknown elsewhere but Swindon was able to provide a solution. Improved design was the answer, coupled with a modification to a two-spindle vertical grinding machine, which was adapted to give a final light finishing cut to both bearings on the connecting rod. Once again, it produced a pair of vital bearings that were precisely in line at precisely the correct centres.

These changes were small and they made no difference to the external appearance of the locomotives, but they had the effect of improving the performance of the machines. Coupled with a carefully-fostered tradition of fine craftsmanship, they ensured that the relatively complex 'Kings' and other four-cylinder locomotives not only went out of the works in perfect order, but remained that way for long

periods, and the class gained a reputation for sweet running. At a time when many locomotives clanked their way around the lines, the GWR four-cylinder engines ran, it was said, like sewing machines.

There was one change in the late 1930s that was obvious. This was the 'streamline' era, and both the LNER and LMS were producing new locomotives with elaborate housings calculated to reduce drag. The GWR got into the act.

However, no new locomotive was designed for, unlike the northern lines, there was no great need for any such development on the GWR. A 'Castle' and 'King' were modified instead. The locomotive so afflicted was No 6014, *King Henry VII*. The result was hideous, a bulbous nose, elaborate fairings around the cylinders and steam pipes, cowlings behind the chimney and safety valve, a V-front cab and continuous splashers. There is a Swindon legend that, faced with the Board's request for a streamlined locomotive, Collett took a paperweight model from his desk and applied lumps of modelling clay. It is unlikely that the project was approached in such a casual fashion, but it is

'The Merchant Venturer' in June 1960 being led by King No 6028 *King George VI* with full steam pressure.

probable that a mock-up was produced in this manner. As a matter of interest, anyone wishing to produce a model of the streamlined *King Edward VII* has only to take a commercial body moulding and apply quantities of epoxy body filler.

Most of the encumbrances were soon discovered to have no great virtue, and were a positive nuisance when it came to preparing the locomotive for traffic. Not surprisingly, as soon as the operating department was able to announce that there were no discernible savings and the publicity department had analysed the many letters of complaint, the majority of fairings were quietly removed and lost. The continuous splashers and V front cab alone remained to show that No 6014 was ever afflicted in this way. In this condition it looked quite pleasing, and this modification is recommended to modellers who would like to add a little variety to their miniature studs.

It has been pointed out that 'Kings' were normally rostered on the heaviest trains where their extra power was best employed. Their potential for high speed was never fully exploited until in 1935, to mark the centenary of the railway, the GWR introduced a new service over the original London & Bristol line.

The 'Bristolian', as the new train was called, was to have had a 90 minute schedule for the 118 mile (190 km) journey, but in the event it was decided to settle for a 105 minute schedule. Initially the train was taken by 'Kings', but with a normal load of only seven coaches, including one of the new buffet cars, the service was passed over to 'Castles'. This did nothing to enhance the reputation of the 'Kings', but the number of people who wanted to travel non-stop from Bristol to London and back again did not justify a longer train. With hindsight, one can see that what was needed was a regular high-speed service between the cities, exploiting the full power of the 'Kings' in conjunction with the superb alignment of Brunel's main line, for the snag with the crack trains of the 1930s was that it was just bad luck if they didn't happen to run when you wanted them. Admittedly the 'Bristolian' was timed to allow the London businessman to spend a useful working day in Bristol. He would arrive at Temple Meads in good time to meet before lunch, and have until about 5.30 to discuss business. It did not seem to occur to the commercial department that there were probably far more Bristol businessmen who needed to visit London!

It was not unknown for a 'King'

to be deliberately rostered on a light train; this was mainly the running in turns, but on occasions a special train would justify the use of a crack locomotive. Such an occasion happened on 29 November 1934 when H.R.H. Princess Marina of Greece married the Duke of Kent. The royal couple travelled from Paddington to Birmingham, Snow Hill, on the first part of their honeymoon. The special train consisted of five coaches, including the Royal Saloon – one of the GWR's own answers to the Pullman car – and the Special Saloon 'King George', now the property of the Dart Valley Railway Association. The newly-married couple had the smaller of the two saloons decorated for their use and in addition the nearest coupe compartment was also filled with flowers. The *Daily Telegraph* reporter stated that it left some seventeen and a half minutes late, but *King George V* was able to make up twelve of these on the 110 minute schedule. Signal checks probably had something to do with the failure to make up all lost time, as five coaches were no load at all for a 'King'.

BR Pacific No 70019 'Lightning' allocated to the Western Region behind No 6010 *King Charles I* in 'The Cornish Riviera Limited' at Aller Junction in July 1956.

The War Years

For the Great Western, World War II started two days early. On 1 September 1939, schoolchildren were evacuated from the London area and the GWR bore the brunt of the load. The normal timetables were completely suspended and only limited local services were provided. Every locomotive and coach that was available in the London area was pressed into service, and the expertise that Old Oak Common had acquired over the years was used to deal with the crisis. Needless to say, none of those involved had the faintest idea where they would end up, let alone the time of arrival; indeed, one suspects that often the train crew were also uncertain.

Except for the fact that 'Kings' were used in the services, this has little to do with their story, but the evacuation marked the end of an era. When, a few days later, the stock was in more or less the right place, wartime austerity was laid over the services. Restaurant cars were taken out of service, speeds were cut and once the belated holidaymakers returned the railways settled down to deal with a completely different pattern of traffic.

There was plenty of opportunity for the 'Kings' to show their power, for trains grew longer, and were loaded more heavily. On most long-distance services, passengers became resigned to having to squeeze in where they could, and it became normal practice to have to stand in the corridor. This was particularly so at weekends, when servicemen and servicewomen used their passes to snatch a few hours at home.

For the first year there was little discernible difference in their outward appearance and although older locomotives became a trifle unkempt as staff shortages grew, the 'Kings', as befitted the

Company's top-flight locomotives, remained resplendent, with all brightwork polished; but there were changes. The side windows were sheeted over to assist blackout, whilst tarpaulins were rigged along the rear of the cab roof so that, at night, they could be drawn back to the tender to prevent enemy aircraft from spotting the glimmer of light as the firedoor was opened.

In 1941 C.B. Collett retired, and was succeeded by F.W. Hawkesworth. At the same time a new livery was adopted. The coaches became brown all over and the locomotives lost their lining, although the principal passenger classes remained green and the 'Kings' copper cap was usually polished.

There is little to report in the way of performance during the war years since there was little opportunity for anything but plain, slogging work. Poor timekeeping was frequent because the lines were crowded with freight; overcrowded trains inevitably led to longer station stops and, above all, the hand-picked coal of pre-war years had gone for good.

The most interesting wartime development was the scheme for the post-war super-power. This was to have been a magnificent Pacific, with a 'King' front end, 6 ft 3 in (1.9 m) wheels, a wide firebox, domed boiler and 280 psi pressure, once again giving the highest tractive effort of any British passenger locomotive. It was not to be, but the boiler pressure and the wheel diameter were used in the 4-6-0 two-cylinder 'Counties' which were authorised by the Ministry because they were mixed-traffic engines. It was a dismal period.

The immediate post-war period was little better. The railways remained under government control and with Labour in power nationalisation was in the air. Any thought of a new design was ruled out, and more 'Castles' were put into production to replace the

aging 'Stars' and 'Saints'. There was no question of more 'Kings', even though train loadings had materially increased. This was because in the post-war period holidays with pay became standard. The majority of workers were much better off than in pre-war days and whereas for most Londoners in the 1930s, a holiday in Devon was as remote a possibility as a visit to the West Indies is today, it was now a perfectly practical proposition, for most fares had been pegged during the war.

There was no alternative to the train. Few people owned cars and petrol was rationed. Long-distance coaches were few and of poor quality and the roads were old-fashioned and tortuous. Soon, the pre-war summer Saturday began to look peaceful in comparison to its post-war equivalent.

The GWR had introduced train reporting numbers in 1934. The purpose was simple, to provide signalmen with an easy means of identifying a train. The need became apparent when it was discovered that nearly all traffic to Cornwall and Devon had to pass over a bottleneck which extended from Norton Fitzwarren to Aller Junction, just west of Newton Abbot. To make matters worse, between Exeter and Cowley Bridge Junction the same two tracks had to carry the Southern Railway's traffic.

Trains converged on this section from all directions and inevitably it became a matter of first come, first served. There were further complications. On the Torquay and Kingswear line, roughly half the long-distance trains stopped at Paignton, but there was no turntable there. There was one at Kingswear, capable of handling 'Kings', but from Goodrington onwards the line was single and worked to capacity. There were no paths for light engines. As often as not, locomotives were exchanged at Newton Abbot, and it was not at all unusual to find that your train finished the last section of its journey behind a pair of locomotives proceeding tender first. In all this chaos, the only way the signalmen could know which trains were which was the reporting number. It is significant that they were not used during the normal weekday services.

To the lay observer, these heavy loadings seemed to cry out for the extra power of the 'Kings', and with a distinct falling off in their performance the idea grew that there was something not quite right about them. There was a natural reaction to the fervent propaganda from the Paddington publicity office, which added to the unease. Then we began to learn the truth: apparently the 'Kings' did not like post-war coal, for as the mines became mechanised, the coal came in smaller chunks and seemed far less effective in the GWR narrow firebox. It was said that the 'Kings' gave more trouble than most.

No one realised that their best years were to come.

Accidents

The Great Western Railway prided itself on its excellent accident record. To any Great Western man, this was the result of first class equipment coupled with careful operating practices. Others spoke of undeserved luck. Whichever it was, the GWR was certainly more inclined to introduce improved equipment, in particular its early electro-mechanical cab signalling device which it termed, with sublime disregard to accuracy, Automatic Train Control. It certainly wasn't automatic and it didn't control trains; it was only a forerunner of the present AWS (advanced warning system) used on British Railways. At best it had a marginal effect on safety, but it did

enable drivers to proceed with greater confidence in fog and falling snow and was justified on this consideration alone.

In view of the undoubted immunity from accidents enjoyed by the line, it is ironic that both accidents leading to a loss of life during the grouping period involved 'Kings', though in neither case was the locomotive itself to blame. If anything, this serves to underline a feature of railway accidents in general: they are so infrequent that no valid conclusions can be drawn from the surrounding situation. This applies with particular force to the two incidents related here, both of which were precipitated by human error.

In any discussion of accidents relating to 'Kings' one should briefly mention the derailment of the leading bogie of No 6003, *King George IV*, when heading the down 'Cornish Riviera' on 10 August 1927. As related earlier, this was attributed to the arrangement of the bogie springs which were subsequently modified. Another relatively important mishap which was even less obvious to the outsider occurred to No 6009, *King Charles II,* which broke its tyre on the 4.15 pm Paddington-Plymouth service, via Bristol. The tyre broke with a loud bang just before entering Box Tunnel and the driver noticed the resultant rough riding. However, when he stopped at Bath, Murphy's Law intervened and the break, stopped at the top of the splasher, was not noticed. A

further inspection at Bristol again revealed nothing, and it was not until Taunton was reached that the gap had opened sufficiently for it to be spotted. The Gibson ring fastenings had kept the tyre in place, and averted a disaster, but it was no wonder that others spoke of the Great Western's luck in such matters.

Certainly, the consequences could have been extremely serious, for had the rim separated or a second break occurred a derailment would have been the least that could have happened. No one was prepared to rely on luck and it was decided that in future the minimum thickness that must remain on 'King' and 'Castle' tyres after tread turning would be raised from 2 in (5 cm) to 2⅛ in (5.3 cm). Another development following these troubles was a modification to the Works weightable, where the adjustment of the springs was checked to ensure that the correct weight was being carried. A section of one rail was machined away and filling pieces provided so that it could be set for level, ½ in (1.3 cm) or 1½ in (3.8 cm) drop, to test statically the effect of a dropped rail on any specific pair of axles. This was a valuable way of discovering whether the axleboxes were doing their job before the locomotive went into service.

Mechanical arrangements and safety devices can only take

Autumn in South Devon. A rather dirty King No 6021 hauls a Paignton-bound train of mixed stock in September 1959.

matters so far however, and increasingly through the twentieth century, railway accidents have been the result of human error, in most cases simple inattention at a crucial moment. The two accidents to be described fall into this category. The first reveals how it was necessary for several small errors to accumulate in order to cause disaster.

It happened in the early hours of 15 January 1936. A down mineral train, headed by a standard 2-8-0 locomotive, was approaching Shrivenham. There it was due to be diverted onto the up goods to allow the up Penzance sleeper to overtake. It was a simple procedure, for the GWR had stopped backing freight trains into lie-by sidings wherever possible, preferring to go to the extra expense of equipping the loops with facing point entries, usually under the command of an extra block post. It must never be forgotten that much of the GWR revenue came from South Wales coal traffic, but this was never allowed to interfere with the more spectacular passenger trains.

As was normal at the time, the train was made up of loose coupled, unbraked mineral wagons, with a Toad – the standard GWR goods brake – at the rear. The main reason why British railways adhered to this old fashioned method was that it was economical. But there was one inherent danger, a sudden jerk could cause a coupling chain to part, and this is what happened to the mineral train. The last three wagons and the Toad were left behind, just short of the approach track circuit governing the Shrivenham home signal. In itself this was not dangerous, for there were two rules that should have protected the train. The first and most important was the red tail lamp.

This small fitting is a vital part of railway operation for with a few significant exceptions, generally multiple-unit stock which cannot accidentally divide without breaking the control circuits, trains carry a loose-fitted lamp, at this time always oil-lit. It was placed on the last vehicle by the guard and its sole purpose was to indicate to the signalman that the train was complete. It had no other real value for under normal conditions, by the time an overtaking driver saw the red light, it was far too late to do anything but pray.

The other precaution lay in the rule which stated that if the train parted, the guard had to protect his rear, in other words take his red lamp, red flag and a number of detonators and walk back along the line, placing detonators at a prescribed distance back, alert for any sign of an oncoming train, until he reached the signal box in the rear.

By a mischance, as the incomplete mineral train passed Shrivenham box, a down train of milk empties was passing. The signalman believed he had seen the tail lamp on the Aberdare coal train. At 5.18 am he accepted the Penzance sleeper.

The down 'Cornish Riviera Limited' hauled by King No 6016 emerging from one of the Teignmouth Tunnels in July 1951.

The coal train ran a short way along the main line to Ashbury Crossing to be diverted onto the goods loop. This box was at the other end of Shrivenham Station, and provided a second chance for the breakaway to have been noticed. Even though the Shrivenham signalman had accepted the express there was just time, had he been informed that the train was broken, to have sent 'obstruction danger' and stopped the express. But at the crucial moment, the Ashbury Crossing signalman was called to the telephone.

He was unsure about the tail lamp, but saw what he took to be a white lamp, a signal from the guard. However, he was sufficiently concerned to look along the line, but seeing the line clear to Shrivenham box, he assumed that all was well. He gave train out of section at 5.18.

Four minutes later, Shrivenham received the 'train entering section' signal from Marston Crossing. The Penzance sleeper had now entered the block section.

In the meantime, the guard had assumed the train was stopped at the Shrivenham home signal. He knew the line well and although the Toad had actually stopped a little short of the position it would have occupied had the driver drawn up to the signal, it was a dark morning and the train might well have stopped short. It was only nine minutes before he realised he had broken away, but these were crucial minutes. Although he immediately put the rule into operation, he had no time to get far enough along the line before the sleeper, headed by No 6007, *King William III* was upon the obstruction.

Most of the force of the obstruction was taken by the Toad, which was driven on to the three rear wagons, forming a solid heap of wreckage into which the train piled. The two leading wagons were thrown clear and propelled forward past Shrivenham box,

alerting the signalman to the tragedy. He immediately sent obstruction danger to the boxes in either direction, thus averting any further damage.

However, nothing could be done for the express. The locomotive turned on its side and the two leading coaches were shattered against the tender. The remaining vehicles were steel-framed and remained intact. Fortunately casualties were light; the driver and one passenger were killed, ten passengers were seriously injured.

It is clear that there was just one element of luck: the breaking away of the two wagons that enabled the Shrivenham signalman to stop a down empty stock train before it ran into the wreck. Two signalmen had failed to note the missing rear lamp, and the guard had been content to sit waiting for an inordinately long time.

The wreck was examined that morning by Collett, who immediately scrapped the locomotive, and arranged for a replacement under Lot 309. Certainly, it appeared to be a very sorry mess. However, when it was lifted up and replaced on the rails, it proved possible to tow it gently to Swindon, where it was stripped down. To everyone's delight, it was found to be in much better condition than at first thought, and when checked by the Zeiss equipment, the largest error in the hornblocks was a matter of 12 thou. Although Cook does not say what was done, this sort of misalignment could be easily put right by regrinding the slides and fitting slightly larger boxes. It turned out to be one of the cheapest Lots ever tackled. The bogie was badly buckled, and when either repaired or replaced, had a slotted front frame. Apparently the idea was to allow more air onto the bearings, though it is doubtful if this had any effect some nine feet back from the obstruction. This odd bogie made its way round several 'Kings' over

the years.

The second accident was much more catastrophic. It happened in the early hours of 4 November 1940, at Norton Fitzwarren, west of Taunton. Today, Norton Fitzwarren only marks the end of the quadruple track, and the junction that leads to what is now the North Somerset Railway. At that time it was a fully-fledged station, with branches to both Minehead and Barnstaple.

The quadruple track extends from Cogload Junction in the east, where the cut-off lines through Westbury rejoin Brunel's original main line through Bristol to Exeter. A little way beyond Norton Fitzwarren is the start of the climb up to Whiteball summit, and it was along this stretch that *City of Truro* put up a speed which, according to which authority you favour, was either just above, or just below, 100 mph.

Although originally the junction at Cogload was on the flat, it was turned into a flyover, the down line from Bristol passing over the new main line. When the tracks through Taunton were quadrupled, the down main from Bristol formed the down relief road.

At 9.50 pm on the night of 3 November, the traditional down West of England train left Paddington. It consisted of 13 vehicles, one a heavy 12-wheeled sleeping car, and was headed by No 6028, *King George VI*. It was at the time of the blitz, though on this occasion there were no incidents to delay the train. It was a long train, heavily laden, with naval personnel returning from leave to Plymouth adding to the number, for it was the last train out of London. All seats were taken and the corridors were packed as well. It was running via Bristol and lost time steadily.

At 12.50 am, the newspaper train left Paddington. Unlike its counterpart on the Southern, which also left around the same time, it had no passenger accommodation, it was only

loaded to five vans and headed by a King, running on the slightly shorter route through Westbury, approached Cogload Junction eight minutes early. The 9.50 was 68 minutes late.

The Taunton signalman was faced with a decision. The sleeper stopped at Taunton on the relief road, but was normally sent over the crossover on to the up main. He decided that instead he would send it out along the down relief, allowing the newspaper train to overtake.

This was precisely the sort of decision a senior signalman in a junction box was empowered to make, and there is no doubt whatsoever that he made the correct decision. The newspaper train was ahead of time and it was not booked to stop at Taunton, thus it could easily clear the section ahead of the late-running sleeper, which could make a slow start along the relief road and, once it was clear of the junction, get away up the bank. The train, although heavy, was well within the capacity of a 'King', and even if it lost a little time up the bank, well, it had lost plenty already. If it preceded the newspaper train, then that would be held up for the

entire distance to Plymouth.

Accordingly, he cleared the down main for the newspaper train, then pulled off the starting signal for the down relief. The sleeper left at 3.44 am, the newspaper train passed through at 3.45, travelling at an estimated 55 mph. With a 'King' at the front and only five vans behind, in all probability it was gently accelerating. It is two miles from Taunton to Norton Fitzwarren.

As the newspaper train cleared the junction, the guard was startled as the window of his van shattered, and he was hit by a flying object. Fearing some damage to his train, he applied the vacuum brake and the train came to a halt beyond the next box, Victory Siding. There he had a conference with the driver and fireman, but an inspection revealed no damage (they clearly missed the van sides, and concentrated on the underframe). They proceeded cautiously to Wellington, where they learned what had happened.

At the subsequent inquiry the driver of the 9.50 sleeping car express said that he believed he had been diverted, as normal, to the down main, and had received

No 6028 *King George VI* and No 6924 *Grantley Hall* running parallel near Goring on a frosty January day in 1959.

and cancelled a warning from the ATC gear as he passed the down relief distant signal controlled by Silk Mill Crossing Box which, for a crossover move, would have remained at caution. He then drove on, reading the signals for the down main which, for most of the distance were set not on the left of the track, as was normal, but on the right. He then passed through Norton Fitzwarren on the relief road, unaware that the station buildings were on the wrong side, and it was not until he was passed by the newspaper train that he realised his error. This happened about 300 yards short of the trap points at the end of the relief road, he had been accelerating and had reached about 45 mph. He seems to have reacted slowly, and was still travelling at about 40 mph when he ran out of road and dived into the soft ground. By this time, the newspaper train had overtaken him far enough for the final van to be alongside. The object that struck the guard proved to be one of the rivets from the 'King's' leading bogie. The sides of the two rear vans of the newspaper train were scored by the ballast thrown up by the derailment.

The fireman of the 9.50 and 26 passengers were killed and a further 56 were seriously injured. The driver clambered out, and a little later appeared at Silk Mill Crossing Box, where he was reported to be 'agitated and dazed'.

Although the subsequent inquiry placed a great deal of emphasis on his statements, it is dangerous to do so. It is equally misleading to suggest that his attention had fallen off because he had been bombed out of his home two nights before. He had been driving the train for some six hours on a dark and stormy night, with no glimmer of light from the surrounding countryside. Under these circumstances, it is perfectly possible for anyone to become disorientated. But we cannot really place any reliance on what he said when we consider that he had climbed out of his locomotive at Norton Fitzwarren Junction, and crossed a fairly wide rhine in the dark, tramped along waterlogged fields and went straight past Norton Fitzwarren signal box! 'Dazed' was an understatement.

By simple calculation it is possible to confirm that the two trains passed as stated above, whilst the approximate speed of the 9.50 is confirmed by the statement of the Norton Fitzwarren signalman, who said it went through at what he believed to be too high a speed for a train that would have to stop.

What is difficult to reconcile is the statement of the 9.50's driver that he received and cancelled the ATC warning at Taunton, but did not receive one at the Norton Fitzwarren distant, as he undoubtedly should have done, for all equipment was checked after the crash, and found to be in good order.

O.S. Nock states that it is possible that the down Silk Mills Crossing distant ATC ramp gave a

The up 'Cornish Riviera' on the sea front at Dawlish hauled by King No 6012 *King Edward VI* in 1951.

Running in King No 6025 *King Henry III* with a light B Set on the Goring water troughs in January 1954.

false danger signal, possibly through dirty contacts. It is equally possible that the Silk Mills Crossing signalman had not had time to clear the distant, for he had had two trains offered almost simultaneously and would have given priority to the down main. Therefore although the Inspecting Officer dismissed the possibility of error here, it is feasible that the driver did imagine he had been put on to the main line. It is equally possible that he was aware of this, but somehow forgot where he was after leaving Taunton, where he was apparently alert, misread the signals and in an abstracted state cancelled the ATC warning that should have alerted him. We can never know.

What is equally puzzling is the

fact that the crew of the newspaper train were unaware that they were overtaking the sleeper close to the junction. Their cab was shrouded with tarpaulins in accordance with blackout regulations, whilst the sleeping car train would be similarly shuttered, but there would have been a change in the sound. The driver of the sleeper, in an abstracted state, was immediately alerted by their passage, yet they had taken over a minute to pass the other train. On reflection, one cannot help feeling that the main cause was the blackout itself. The crash has often been held up as an example of the GWR's extraordinary luck, for had the newspaper train been just one minute later, it would have ploughed into the wreckage.

Resurgence

When the nationalised British Railways was formed in January 1948, the problem of reorganising the system was swept quietly under the carpet. Six regions were formed in England and Wales and, subject only to a few boundary adjustments, they were the original companies. Superficially, apart from a coat of paint, all was much as before.

There was of course the period of the experimental liveries, during which various trains painted in colour schemes that seemed good to those concerned were put into service 'to gauge public opinion'. How this was done remains something of a mystery, since no overt attempt was made to find out what the public thought and most of the schemes sank without trace. The final result was slightly different and for the first time introduced a special livery for the most powerful passenger classes. It was alleged to be Caledonian Blue, but there was not much support for it. The 'Kings' duly appeared in this colour and were said to look hideous. The same was said of the LMS Pacifics, the LNER A4s and the Southern 'Merchant Navys', the blue livery was quietly dropped and all passenger locomotives appeared in BR green. Apart from some slight variation in the lining, this was the old GWR locomotive livery, and as GWR locomotives retained their original numbers and nameplates, the main difference was the appearance of the LMS-style smokebox numerals and the BR heraldic device on the tender. Originally this was a rather emaciated lion straddling a wheel and was rapidly dubbed 'The Ferret and Dartboard'. A later version had the lion crouching in a crown perched on a wheel. It looked faintly apprehensive perhaps because it had a rather prickly seat.

In 1948 the Locomotive Exchanges were staged. The idea was that selected locomotives from each of the former railways would work over other lines under carefully controlled test conditions, ostensibly to determine the future British Railways locomotive designs.

The exchanges were not only the largest, they were far and away the best organised of all British locomotive exchanges, and a great deal of useful information was obtained. However, they were largely viewed as a contest, and ever since there have been attempts to discover "who won".

The 'Kings' began with a distinct handicap, having been built to take full advantage of the generous Great Western loading gauge, and were only allowed to take part in one series of 'foreign' tests, the Kings Cross–Leeds runs. There was an even more serious handicap, all GWR designs were the earliest in their groups.

Considerable disappointment was experienced when the coal consumption of the GWR locomotives was published. Bearing in mind the excellent pre-war figures the drop was dramatic and of course it was said that the wrong coal had been used. All who looked on the exchanges as a sporting contest murmured 'foul', but the engineers who studied the test results gleaned a lot of useful information from the results. They discovered that for high power output under post-war conditions, a wide firegrate was preferable. Swindon, in its aborted Pacific design, had already come to this conclusion.

The real lesson of the exchanges was that exchange trials were almost useless as a means of determining the everyday performance of a locomotive. The trial locomotives were manned in a wholly artificial fashion and the visiting crew were at the disadvantage of not knowing the road. This was not just a handicap in a contest, it was a more serious obstruction to the underlying aim: discovering just how the locomotive performs under both normal and optimum conditions.

The exchanges showed up some broad conclusions, and so far as the 'King' class was concerned these were that it was a remarkably good design, but showing its age. This was quite important, since it was the most powerful machine available on the Western Region and was destined to hold this distinction down to the end of steam.

Fortunately, better test procedures were to hand. In Churchward's day the GWR had produced a static testing plant. In its original form it could only absorb 500 hp and became of little use other than as a way of running a locomotive in after repairs or when new. Under Collett, it had been upgraded and was able to test any GW locomotive at its maximum output.

At the same time, under Sam Ell, the Western devised an improved method of road testing, where the boiler was worked at a continuous high output. During these tests some enormous loads were shifted over relatively short distances, with two firemen on the footplate to spell each other. The idea was to assess the maximum power output a locomotive could produce, and then to see if it could be improved.

In the case of the 'Kings' it most certainly could. As has been pointed out, it was a fairly old design, and in one respect was rather behind the times, even for 1927. When in the early years of the century Churchward had applied superheat to his locomotives, he adopted a fairly low degree. At the time there were many good reasons for this.

Superheating is a means of boosting the potential power output of steam at a given pressure, because although the actual work is done by steam pressure, the amount of expansion

The 'Welsh Marches Pullman' hauled by No 6000 *King George V* crosses Cefn-Mawr viaduct on the return trip from Chester in August 1983.

that can take place is governed by the total heat of the steam. This is no place for even a brief excursion into the complexities of thermodynamics and what follows is a simplification. Superheat performs two useful functions. First, by providing a margin of heat over and above that needed to turn the water into steam, it prevents condensation in the engine; secondly, by packing more energy into a given mass of steam it allows that steam to perform more useful work.

Although on other railways relatively high superheat was adopted to allow small locomotives to produce more work, and enable them to haul heavy trains at higher speeds, the Churchward 4-6-0s had enough margin of power in their original, unsuperheated form to handle most duties. As with all improvements, superheating has

its drawbacks, one of which is that the steam is not only much hotter but it is also completely dry. Lubrication therefore becomes of even greater importance, and in the early years of the century oil technology was unable to cope. It was not because there were problems in keeping the cylinders lubricated, more oil could always be forced in by means of a simple pump, the well-known mechanical lubricator. The trouble was that the oil was carbonised and it was necessary to dismantle the valves and scrape carbon deposits off the rings at frequent intervals. The low superheat adopted by Churchward and standardised on the GWR avoided this problem; indeed, adequate lubrication was ensured by the cab-mounted hydrostatic lubricator which, with its visual feed, was greatly loved by the enginemen.

By 1927 better oils were available, but Swindon remained firmly convinced that low superheat was less bother, and performed well enough for their locomotives. But by 1940 doubts had set in, for when Stanier took low superheat to the LMS, the results were anything but happy.

So the 'Kings', along with other GWR locomotives, received modified boilers containing more rows of superheating elements, and mechanical lubricators appeared on the running boards. The improvement was marked.

Another change took place at the exhaust end of the cycle. From the outset the GWR practice had been good, the importance of a free exhaust and correctly-proportioned blast-pipe and petticoat pipe, in relation to smokebox volume was well understood. Right to the end of steam, it was largely an empirical matter, for although most of the factors are capable of being expressed mathematically, the interactions are so complex that in our present state of knowledge, it is impossible to devise a thoroughly reliable formula which will predict the end results. Preferred relationships were established instead on the basis of controlled tests or, putting it crudely, by organised trial and error.

In this respect, the design team at Swindon were clearly ahead of all other centres, and the small team led by Sam Ell had got things down to a fine art. They became the official trouble shooters for British Railways; if any class of locomotive refused to steam properly they were called in, and invariably were able to devise simple and relatively inexpensive methods of curing the problem permanently.

When it came to the 'Kings' the matter was not quite so simple, for they were not starting from the benchmark of a poor design, but from one which in its day was as good as any in the world. The initial trials of twin blastpipes were inconclusive, and it was not until the late 1950s that the arrangement was standardised.

The combination of high superheat and twin blastpipes almost brought the 'Kings' up to modern standards. It has been said with some truth that complete internal streamlining was not attempted; that would have involved radical changes such as a completely redesigned set of cylinders and valve chests.

At this point, we have to look at commercial considerations. High superheat was not too difficult to arrange, for the GWR boilers were

designed for easy interchange. New blastpipes were again not too difficult to fit into normal maintenance schedules, for it has to be realised that in the hot and dirty conditions of a smokebox, wear on the cast-iron parts is appreciable, but the parts involved are relatively cheap to produce, since there is very little machining involved. The cost, spread over the projected life of the locomotives, was reasonable. On the other hand, new cylinders would cost more than they were worth. One must remember that they were very good cylinders to begin with.

The modifications rejuvenated the 'Kings'. Similar alterations improved the 'Castles', with the result that from the mid-1950s until the final demise of steam, Western Region expresses were competently handled. Despite the fact that the coal put into the tenders would have resulted in a general loss of performance in pre-war days, not only were schedules maintained, but it proved possible to tighten the timings over several routes. As in pre-war days, the 'Kings' were regularly rostered on the heaviest trains and despite the fact that they were now thirty years old, seemed as good as new.

They looked different. The double chimney didn't help, in its early stages, it was a very awkward-looking built-up arrangement. Although it made absolutely no difference to the performance, the Swindon drawing office under the direction of the new Chief, Smeddle, who had been transferred from Darlington, produced a more elegant design, with slightly curved sides. There was a faint North Eastern influence to be discerned, though whether that had anything to do with the fact that Mr Smeddle originally came from Darlington is not easy to determine. The two styles were not dissimilar.

A subtle change took place with the steam pipes, for here the movement of the outside cylinders

began to produce cracks. This trouble was cured by increasing the sweep of the curves and eliminating the former central straight portion, thus giving even greater flexibility. The casing over the centre cylinders valve chests was altered as the inevitable front-end renewals took place, and the mechanical lubricators were quite prominent. But the 'Kings' still looked much as they always had, timeless, immutable. They had always been there; indeed, there were few observers of the railway scene in the 1950s who could clearly remember when there had been no 'Kings'. It was impossible to conceive the Western without them.

Right to the end, they turned in a good performance. Logs of the period reveal that as in the past even with heavy trains, they had enough in hand to maintain start-to-stop timings, even when brought to a standstill by adverse signals. Speeds in the middle to high seventies were still commonplace.

Into the bargain, throughout the 1950s the 'Kings' remained resplendent. Regrettably this came to an end. As more and more diesel-hydraulic locomotives become available, and as the 'Western' diesels took over the workings once reserved for 'Kings', they became scruffy; and worse was to follow.

At one time name and number plates could be bought as scrap, few people bothered to even pay the few pounds they cost. After all they were rather big items. In the 1960s all that changed, their value as memorabilia became clear and inevitably the unscrupulous, dishonest individual moved in. Plates were stolen, and in order to circumvent the activities of the thieves, British Railways removed name and numberplates wholesale, and for the final months, the proud 'Kings' ran out their days in a filthy condition, with chalked numbers on their cab sides. It was a sorry end to a fine career.

What If...?

It is a great temptation, when surveying any locomotive class to ask oneself, with the benefit of hindsight, what might have happened if only ...? In most cases, such speculation is futile, however in the case of the 'Kings' there was one special condition that rarely applied: a degree of pressure was applied to construct a new, more powerful locomotive in a great hurry for purely propaganda purposes. What if that pressure had not been applied, what if the development had been allowed to take a more natural course?

The 'Castles' were a complete success and were only slightly extended but not outclassed on a few trains. Extra power in the sense of tractive effort was not essential, the locomotives really needed to be able to deliver a higher output at high speeds. There was to hand an effective method, one which later did precisely that – high superheat. It would have been simple and relatively cheap to have produced a high-superheat No 8 boiler in 1926/7 and to have equipped six to eight 'Castles' with these boilers for the summer of 1927. As for the Fair of the Iron Horse, a 'Castle' would have had exactly the same impact on the USA, and the self-same publicity could have been generated.

Work could then have proceeded in a more leisurely fashion towards the next step forward in motive power, and providing the design office was informed that the civil engineers were working towards a 22 ton axle load, the new class could have been drawn up for that standard. With more time to reflect, the options of a 4-6-2 or even a 4-8-0 could have been explored.

There would be more than just a possible change of wheel formula. The locomotive would have had high superheat from the outset. Given the existing interest in draughting in Swindon, it is possible that in 1935-6 the new locomotive would have had a better smokebox arrangement. It is more than probable that some degree of improved steam passage design might have been incorporated. Furthermore, and this is perhaps the most important factor, this new locomotive could have changed the plans of the Board in other respects. What if, instead of applying the Government grants of the 1930s to an abortive cut-off at Teignmouth, and a useless branch to Looe, the GWR had undertaken a massive bridge-strengthening programme to bring super-power to all its principal routes?

There is another fascinating speculation; by the 1930s the Great Western had lost interest in establishing speed records. What if they had decided to take up *Mallard*'s challenge?

It is not difficult to picture. A Sunday afternoon in late 1937; the place, Exeter St. Davids. Standing in Platform 5 is a short train, the dynamometer car, two first-class coaches and one of the new buffet cars; at the head, resplendent after a very careful check at Swindon, No 6000 *King George V*. Representatives of the press and a number of notable amateurs are present, headed by Cecil J. Allen. The line ahead has been specially cleared, and although there are plenty of platelayers waiting, they will be standing on the down side of the line. There will be no repetition of the trouble with *City of Truro.*

The special train takes it out of Exeter, but by the time Stoke Cannon is passed *King George V* is well into its stride. The climb to Whiteball is taken smartly but, once clear of the tunnel, everything is opened up. So far, we are on safe ground. A powerful, fast running, locomotive with a light train is heading down the GWR's traditional romping stretch. It is going to go very fast, but there will be ample time to slow down to a sensible speed before Norton Fitzwarren, let alone Taunton. There is no doubt that the locomotive would have had no problem raising a good head of steam, or that the motion would have given any trouble, for the improved bearings had taken care of the problems other lines were experiencing with their most powerful passenger locomotives. There is just one small, niggling, doubt. Would *King George V,* on the day, have surpassed *Mallard*'s record speed?

In all probability, that was why it was never tried.

An up Fishguard Express in Sonning Cutting in September 1960 behind No 6009 *King Charles II.*

The End

All the 'Kings' were withdrawn in 1962. To anyone who loved the steam locomotive, it was not a moment too soon. Dirty, unkempt, bereft of both name and numberplates, to thwart the activities of unofficial collectors who had stolen far too many valuable relics already, they were staggering out their final hours, surrounded by hordes of diesel hydraulics. It is slightly ironic to think that the obsequies of the 'Kings' were nowhere near those that attended the demise of the 'Westerns', yet the 'Kings' came into service before most enthusiasts who saw the end were born. Those who waved farewell to the diesel hydraulics had seen them come.

The first 'King' No 6006, went in February; then there was a lull until seven went in June, and a further three in July. No withdrawals took place during August, but in September thirteen went, leaving just six. Two more were taken out of service in November, the final four, including No 6000, *King George V*, were written off in December.

Well, almost.

King George V was scheduled for preservation and for a long while lingered in a shed in Swindon. Like so many others earmarked for retention, there seemed no place for this famous locomotive. Then British Transport bowed to the inevitable, and realised that there was a greater likelihood that the lines closed by Beeching and his successors might reopen, than that funds would be available for the sort of museum that could house more than a fraction of the collection. Those individuals who had a suitable site and who were prepared to house and look after the relics could have them on loan.

The conditions were strict and few could meet them, but one was found in the unlikely shape of Bulmers. They had bought a train of true Pullman cars and were housing them under cover on their own lines. Moreoever, their siding was long enough to allow some movement. They applied for the King of Locomotives – and got it.

In 1968 *King George V* went to Hereford amid a blaze of publicity. To be truthful he – for this machine has a personality – is a marvel of transplant surgery, parts from many 'Kings' have gone into his restoration, which fittingly makes him representative of the class. With the return of steam-hauled specials, *King George V* has been seen on BR metals on many occasions, hauling both the Bulmers' train and the Great Western Society's preserved GWR set. Of course, as befits a retired gentleman, *King George V* no longer attempts speed records, and is content to show another generation why steam has an appeal that diesels and electrics lack.

Above: The might and majesty of the 'King' class is well illustrated in this view of the preserved *King George V.*

Left: Up express from Weston-Super-Mare heading for Paddington in May 1960, passing Sonning Cutting headed by No 6006.

Far left: King George V, as preserved in November 1980, leaves Shrewsbury for Chester with 'The Zenith' Special including Bulmers' preserved Pullman Cars.

The Kings: Modelling Notes

Despite the clear popularity of the class among enthusiasts from all walks of life, it is incredible that before the war no 'off the peg' models were available. This is not quite so alarming as it sounds to modern ears, for in the inter-war period, most quality models were batch-produced by craftsmen rather than mass produced from moulds. As a result, it was possible to order a locomotive of one's choice for a small percentage more than one paid for a listed model, and occasionally this led to another type being included in the catalogue, marked 'to special order only'.

It should of course be stressed that these models were, by today's standards, extremely expensive. A Bassett-Lowke locomotive cost anything from £1.17.6 to four guineas for a clockwork version. At a time when a craftsman on a standard 48-hour week took home around £3.10s.0d this represents about £60 to £120 in today's money.

The first mass-produced 'King' was produced by Graham Farish in 4-mm scale. The model had a diecast body, and was a fair, though poorly-proportioned replica, and was further hampered by being fitted with an extremely ingenious motor in the tender. On a fair day this might possibly pull the skin off a rice pudding, but in most cases it functioned so erratically as to damn the range, even if the brittle plastic wheels, apt to loose their flanges, were not a sufficient disincentive.

It was not until the late 1970s, after the class had vanished, that a mass-produced model appeared, when, to make up for the lapse three turned up in quick succession. The first was an unpainted brass model which originated in the Far East, and was produced to the order of Fulgurex, the well-known Swiss concern. Although the model is superb mechanically and its basic dimensions are correct, there are many subtle errors which offend the knowledgeable, and in view of the high price – around £150 at the outset and rising rapidly with inflation until the relatively small batch was sold – it did not find favour with the enthusiast.

This was largely because of the appearance of the Lima version which, whilst containing some errors, was slightly more accurate than the Fulgurex model and if one wanted a King for operating purposes you could buy the complete class from Lima for very little more than one Fulgurex model!

Shortly after the Lima 'King', Hornby produced one. Again there were some errors and although the initial model was tender powered, it had the skirted boiler that was initially used to hide the motor. This was quickly rectified and the latest version, with a full boiler and some additional detail, is acceptable for the purely operating layout.

For those wishing to produce a more individual model, Wills Finecast offer a cast kit in 4-mm scale. It is generally much easier to produce a precise model of a specific locomotive when one begins with a kit of parts, and does not first have to dismember a single piece body.

Although no 'King' exists for N gauge, the Graham Farish 'Castle' has a rather large boiler and is to the writer's eye rather nearer a 'King' than its supposed prototype. It should be mentioned that the comments made on the early Farish 00 models do not apply to the modern N gauge stock; the present management, whilst keeping to the Farish principles of producing goods at competitive prices, are no longer apt to cut corners if quality could suffer.

The 'Kings' have long been popular with scratchbuilders, and excellent models have been produced through the years. Although, in 4-mm scale, it seems hardly worth the bother, workers in 7-mm and other less popular scales will wish to consider the class. *Building Model Locomotives* by R.J. Roche & G.G. Templer is an excellent guide, whilst Guy Williams' *Model Locomotive Construction in 4-mm Scale* is an extremely useful book for smaller sizes. Both books are published by Ian Allan.

It is interesting to note that there is a strong parallel between the prototype and model, for although popular with modelmakers, the 'Kings' are less popular with operators. With train lengths restricted by lack of space, it is difficult to justify the use of GWR Super Power on a model layout, and hence the 'Castle' is generally preferred.

Any model locomotive is greatly improved by the addition of etched name and numberplates and with only a class of 30 to cover, all 'Kings' are nominally available from stock, although as engraved plates are only available over the counter in a few selected stores, it is generally necessary to order direct if one requires a specific locomotive. When changing the name of a ready-to-run model in GWR livery, it is essential of course to amend the number on the bufferbeam with correct transfers. For BR condition, engraved matching smokebox plates are included at extra cost in the set.

No	Original Name	Built	Double Chimney	Withdrawn
6000	King George V	6/27	12/56	12/62[4]
6001	King Edward VII	7/27	2/56	9/62
6002	King William IV	7/27	3/56	9/62
6003	King George IV	7/27	7/58	6/62
6004	King George III	7/27	7/58	6/62
6005	King George II	7/27	7/56	11/62
6006	King George I	2/28	6/56	2/62
6007	King William III[1]	3/28	9/56	9/62
6008	King James II	3/28	12/58	6/62
6009	King Charles II	3/28	5/56	9/62
6010	King Charles I	4/28	3/56	6/62
6011	King James I	4/28	3/56	12/62
6012	King Edward VI	4/28	2/58	9/62
6013	King Henry VIII	5/28	6/56	6/62
6014	King Henry VII	5/28	9/57	9/62
6015	King Richard III	6/28	9/55	9/62
6016	King Edward V	6/28	1/58	9/62
6017	King Edward IV	6/28	12/55	7/62
6018	King Henry VI	6/28	3/58	12/62
6019	King Henry V	7/28	4/57	9/62
6020	King Henry IV	5/30	2/56	7/62
6021	King Richard II	6/30	3/57	9/62
6022	King Edward III	6/30	5/56	9/62
6023	King Edward II	6/30	6/57	6/62
6024	King Edward I	6/30	3/57	6/62[5]
6025	King Henry III	7/30	3/57	12/62
6026	King John	7/30	3/58	9/62
6027	King Richard I	7/30	8/56	9/62
6028	King Henry II[2]	7/30	1/57	11/62
6029	King Stephen[3]	8/30	12/57	7/62

[1]No 6007 was nominally withdrawn on 5 March 1936 and renewed on 24 March 1936.
[2]No 6028 was renamed *King George VI* in January 1937.
[3]No 6029 was renamed *King Edward VIII* in May 1936.
[4]Preserved as part of the National Collection.
[5]Privately preserved.

Wheel arrangement:	4-6-0
Cylinders (4) bore and stroke:	16.25 in × 28 in
Driving wheel dia:	6ft 6in
Boiler pressure:	250 lb
Tractive effort @ 75% pressure:	35,400 lb
Total evap. surface:	2,201 sq ft
Grate area:	34.3 sq ft
Superheating surface:	313 sq ft
Boiler dia:	6 ft/5 ft 6 in taper
Coupled wheelbase:	16 ft 3 in
Engine wheelbase:	29 ft 3 in
Max axle load:	22.5 tons
Adhesion weight:	67.5 tons
Total engine weight:	89 tons
Water capacity:	4,000 gal
Coal capacity:	6 tons
Total wheelbase:	57 ft 5½ in
Engine & tender weight:	135.7 tons

Acknowledgements

The author wishes to thank all those who supplied illustrations.
Colour-Rail: all pictures except the following:
British Rail: pp. 5, 15 (btm).
H.C. Casserley: p. 38.
Derek Cross: pp. 32, 37, 43, 45, 46 (btm), 49 (top), 55.
C.J. Freezer: p. 4.
John Marshall: pp. 9, 15 (top), 16 (top), 16 (btm), 26 (btm), 26 (right), 26 (left), 36.
Peter Semmens: p. 12.
W.A. Sharman: pp. 2-3, 28, 30, 31, 40 (btm), 51, endpapers.
Spectrum Colour Library: p. 54.
P. Underhay: p. 54.
C. Walker: 40 (top).